Farm La[bour and the]
Irish S[truggle]
1900–1976

Dan Bradley

ATHOL BOOKS

Farm Labourers: Irish Struggle 1900–1976
is published by

**Athol Books
10 Athol Street
Belfast
BT12 4GX**

ISBN 0 85034 038 1

© **Dan Bradley, 1988**

Much of the material in Chapter 5 has already appeared in **Saothar 11**, journal of the *Irish Labour History Society*, 1986

This book is sold subject to the condition that it shall not be, by way of trade or otherwise, be lent, resold, hired out, or otherwise circulated without the publisher's prior consent in any form of binding or cover other than that in which it is published and without a similar condition including this condition being imposed on the subsequent purchaser

COVER DESIGN: **Pat Pidgeon**

TABLE OF CONTENTS

	Page
Acknowledgements	4
Abbreviations	4
Schedules of Tables and Illustrations	5
Introduction	7
Chapter 1 **Living And Working Conditions**	10
Chapter 2 **Agricultural Labourer Organisations In Co. Cork Prior To 1919**	24
Chapter 3 **The Zenith Of Trade Unionism On The Farm 1919-20**	43
Chapter 4 **The Defeat Of Trade Unionism On The Farm 1921-23**	56
Chapter 5 **The Workers' Union Of Ireland And Federation Of Rural Workers 1944-48**	74
Chapter 6 **The Agricultural Wages Board, 1936-1976**	93
Conclusion	117
Review Of Sources	119
Bibliography	122
Index	127

Acknowledgements

I wish to thank all those who helped in the writing of this book, though none of the people mentioned bears any responsibility for the views expressed or for errors which are contained in the book. Mr. Con Moynihan of Cork proved a very valuable source. Professor Joseph Lee, Department of Modern History, U.C.C., supervised post-graduate research on farm labourers in Ireland. Mr. Patrick Murphy, F.W.U.I., 29 Parnell Square, Dublin 1, kindly granted an interview and provided copies from manuscript material.

I am indebted to the staffs of Cork County Library, Farranlea Road, Cork; Archives Department, U.C.C.; Old Newspaper Section, Cork City Library, the National Library of Ireland; State Paper Office, Dublin Castle.

Special thanks to Pauline Hensey for her support.

Abbreviations

AWB	Agricultural Wages Board
CFA	Cork Farmers' Association
CFU	Cork Farmers' Union
CE	**Cork Examiner**
FRW	Federation of Rural Workers
ICTU	Irish Congress of Trade Unions
IFU	Irish Farmers' Union
IHS	**Irish Historical Studies**
ILLA	Irish Land and Labour Association
IP	**Irish Press**
IT	**Irish Times**
ITGWU	Irish Transport and General Workers' Union
ITJ	**Irish Trade Journal**
ITUC	Irish Trade Union Congress
ILPTUC	Irish Labour Party and Trade Union Congress
JSSISI	**Journal of the Statistical and Social Inquiry Society of Ireland**
KFA	Kildare Farmers' Association
LLA	Land and Labour Association
MCC	Member County Council
NAA	National Agricultural Association
NALU	National Agricultural Labourers' Union
NLI	National Library of Ireland
NUAW	National Union of Agricultural Labourers
RDC	Rural District Council

RIC   Royal Irish Constabulary
SPO   State Paper Office
UIL   United Irish League
WUI   Workers' Union of Ireland

Schedule Of Tables

Table 1	Number of Farmers, Relatives Assisting and Labourers in Each Province, 1926
Table 2	Weekly Budget for a Rural Labourer, Wife and Two Children in North Cork, Spring 1923
Table 3	The Introduction of Tractors and Decline in Permanent Farm Employees, 1951-60
Table 4 (a)	Number of Cottages in 12 Munster and Leinster Counties
Table 4 (b)	Number of Cottages in other Counties of Eire
Table 5	Number of ILLA Branches, 1899-1904
Table 6	Number of Farm Labourers in Co. Cork ITGWU Branches Contrasted with Selected other Branches
Table 7	Total Farm Labourer Membership ITGWU, 30.6.1919
Table 8	Threatened Farm Strikes in Co. Cork, 1919
Table 10	Cork Farm Strikes, 1920
Table 11	Index of Irish Agricultural Wholesale Prices, 1919-21
Table 12	Cost of Living Increase, 1939-44
Table 13	Membership Figures for FRW, July 1947
Table 14	Percentage Change in 3 Factors Related in Determining Relative Positions of Labourers' Wages and Employing Farmers' Incomes, 1924-35
Table 15	Variation in the Wage Rates for Farm Labourers in 1931 and 1935
Table 16	Number of Males (non-family) Employed on Farms, 1927-36, Inclusive of Those Under 18 Years of Age
Table 17	Results of Intervention by AWB, 1937-45

Illustrations

page 23	**A Group of Farm Workers, 1946**
page 38-9	**Map of Co. Cork Dispensary District, 1935**
page 42	**Labour In North Kerry, Report 2.5.1919**
page 46	**Line Torn Up, Train Derailed, Report 18.8.1919**
page 72	**The War Of Labour, Report 22.2.1919**
page 73	**Police Escort For Lord Carew, 27.8.1946**
page 73	**Farm Strikers Gathering, 27.8.1946**
page 92	**Notice of Demonstration, 23.4.1947**

For my mother, and
In memory of my father.

Introduction

In 1971 F.S.L. Lyons noted in **Ireland Since The Famine** (pages 4, 271) that the agricultural labourer of post-Famine Ireland was ignored by historians, as he had been by contemporaries. Since 1971, however, publications by Lee, Donnelly, Hoppen, Bew, Clark, Fitzpatrick, Boyle and O'Shea have thrown much light on the subject (these are listed in the Bibliography, which also contains full details of all works cited in the text). None of those works, however, go beyond 1921, by which year indeed some of them tend to write the farm labourer off completely. Fitzpatrick entitles his article, **The Disappearance of the Irish Agricultural Labourer, 1841-1912.** His contention arises out of the difficulty associated with attempting to define the term, 'agricultural labourer', because by 1900 some who were small holders described themselves as labourers, while labourers with plots were known to return themselves in official statistics as farmers (see, for example, **Census of Population 1926**, Vol VI, p.ix).

The difficulty of definition is dealt with in the present study by describing the agricultural labourer as one engaged mainly or wholly at work related to the functioning of the farm, on an employee basis, for regular monetary recompense, excluding nurserymen, gardeners, forestry workers and those whose work is mainly domestic service.

This definition is sufficiently broad to include four sub-categories of labourer: the 'servant' who 'lived-in' with his employer for a six month or longer period and was paid at the end of the contract; the married worker who lived in a workman's house belonging to the farmer; the worker who lived in a cottage provided under the 1883 and subsequent *Labourers' Acts*; and fourthly, the small holder who worked most of the time for another farmer. The exclusion of those engaged mainly on domestic service implies that the large numbers of people, mostly women, who were employed *in* the houses of farmers are not the subject of this study.

Consequently, little will be said of *women* farm labourers specifically hereafter, as they constituted only 1% of the total, as here defined, in 1926, and less in subsequent years. Similarly the words 'on an employee basis' in the definition implies that the 'relatives assisting' or members of the farmer's family who worked on the land are not included.

Chapter 1 of the study sets out to illustrate that, though labourers constituted only 18% of the agricultural workforce for the 26 counties as a whole in 1926, a different perspective emerges when regional variations are taken into consideration. It is established that labourers were concentrated in twelve counties, south and east of lines joining Dundalk–Limerick City–Bandon. The specific counties to which the findings herein apply are Dublin, Kildare, Meath, Louth, Wicklow, Wexford, Kilkenny, Carlow, Waterford, Tipperary, east Limerick and Cork east of the Bandon–Macroom–Kanturk lines.

Having outlined demographic features *Chapter 1* proceeds to deal with the diet, working conditions, social status and housing of farm labourers during this century.

Professor Joseph Lee has written that, by 1914 "...the crux of the matter was that the rise in the labourer's standard of living lagged behind the rise in his aspirations" (**The Modernisation of Irish Society, 1848-1918**, p.8). The present study demonstrates that such remained the position until the 1960s. The focus is on the various agitations undertaken by labourers to improve their pay, working conditions and social status in society. Cork County is made the subject of intensive study, and developments therein are related to what is known of the pattern of agitation in other counties. In this regard *Chapter 2* surveys farm labourer organisations before 1918. Particular attention is paid to the Irish Land and Labour Association (ILLA) from 1905 onwards, as its split into factions in that year retarded labourer efforts. The emergence of the Irish Transport And General Workers' Union (ITGWU) as a force in rural Ireland and its rivalry with the ILLA factions are then discussed.

Chapter 3 analyses the wave of farm strikes 1919-20. It illustrates that the rural agitation of those years was a combination of militant trade unionism and that agrarian violence which had troubled Ireland periodically since the Whiteboy movement of the 1760s.*

Chapter 4 then examines how the formidable rural organisation of 1920 was defeated in Cork 1921-3, and a comparison made with what is known of similar development in other Munster and Leinster counties. Close attention is paid to the separate and combined effects on the labourers' movement of the final phase of the War of Independence, the agricultural depression and the Civil War.

Chapter 5 explores the revival of trade unionism on the farm under Jim Larkin, 1944-6, and the consequent bitter struggles for better working conditions involving the Federation Of Rural Workers which Larkin helped to found in 1946. Particular attention is paid to the North Kildare farm strike of that year. The burnings, spiking of fields, intimidation, threats of eviction and boycotts of that dispute were more appropriate to nineteenth century Ireland than the mid-twentieth, but serve as a testimony to the neglect felt by the farm labourer.

Chapter 6 outlines how the policy for agriculture of the first Free State government affected farm workers. The decline in the labourers' standard of living which necessitated state intervention and the establishment of the *Agricultural Wages Board* (AWB) in 1936 is described. Finally the procedures and performance of the AWB are analysed.

*(See T.D. Williams (ed.), **Secret Societies In Ireland**; Samuel Clark & James S. Donnelly, Jnr., **Irish Peasants: Violence & Political Unrest 1780-1914**.)

The neglect of the labourer both by contemporaries and historians led to the creation of the myth that his exploits were not recorded. The present study attempts to disprove that belief. Extensive newspaper and other written records of the activities of labourers after 1900 existed but needed to be unearthed. Consequently, the present study is largely an 'archaeological excavation' of the subject.

Finding the correct location to dig proved time consuming. It required exhaustive scrutiny of newspaper files and determined pursuit of 'leads' gleaned from personal interviews with farm labourers in Co. Cork.

In the preface to Anne O'Dowd's **Meitheal — a study of co-operative Labour in Rural Ireland** (Dublin, 1981), Caoimhin O'Danachair has warned that any study which devotes a paragraph to farmers of all grades and the remainder to labourers will inevitably be unbalanced. While accepting that admonition, it is nevertheless necessary to redress the previous imbalance whereby farm labourers were ignored. Furthermore, by illustrating the ruthlessness of some labourers, the present study aims to avoid stereotyping the employees as the paragons of all virtue and the employers as perennial oppressors.

Dan Bradley
June 1988

chapter one

Living And Working Conditions

By 1911 the standard of living of the farm labourer had improved to the extent that the most harrowing features of his predecessors' existence during the immediate post-Famine decades had been alleviated. However he remained alienated from society because his living and working conditions lagged so far behind his aspirations. The following survey indicates the position.

(i) Demographic background

The 1926 census recorded 125,972 agricultural labourers in the Free State excluding nurserymen, gardeners and forestry workers. This however was less than 18% of the total agricultural workforce, as in 1926 there were 268,927 farmers and 262,489 'relatives assisting'.

From such figures little distinct labourer identity would be expected to exist. When regional variations are considered, however, a very different perspective emerges. Farm labourers were concentrated in 12 East Munster and Leinster counties where in each case they constituted about 33% of the farm workforce. A comparison of figures for the provinces indicates the marked contrast.

Table 1. Number Of Farmers, Relatives Assisting And Labourers In Each Province 1926

	Farmers & Relatives Assisting	*Labourers*
Connacht	176,994	11,263
Ulster (3 counties)	84,207	12,784
Leinster	109,620	52,019
Munster (minus Kerry & Clare)	103,097	40,226
Kerry & Clare	59,107	10,041

Census Of Population 1926, Volume 5, p.14-15

Table 1 indicates that Connacht had the biggest number of farmers and relatives assisting, but that labourers were only 6% of the labour force in the province. Similarly, for the three Ulster counties — Donegal, Cavan and Monaghan — only 13% of the total were employees. This contrasts sharply with Leinster where almost 33% of the total were labourers. The inclusion of Clare and Kerry in the total for Munster distorts the concentration of employees east of the Bandon–Limerick City line. When Kerry, Clare, West Cork and West Limerick are excluded the percentage of labourers in the workforce in East Munster is similar to the 33% of Leinster.

At *county* level the 33% ratio is maintained in the twelve counties Dublin, Kildare, Meath, Louth, Wicklow, Wexford, Kilkenny, Carlow, Waterford, Tipperary, Limerick and Cork east of the Bandon–Macroom–Kanturk lines. By 1946 the ratio had not altered significantly. In fact the percentage of labourers in the twelve counties had *increased* slightly because the number of relatives assisting declined more sharply than labourers over those twenty years (see 1946 Census, Vol V, p.16). It was only after 1946 that a new wave of emigration led to a sharp decline in the number of labourers.

Emphasis has been placed on this point concerning the concentration of employees in twelve counties because it was significant in maintaining a strong labourer identity in that region.

An additional factor in maintaining that identity was the pattern of cottage building. Department of Local Government and Public Health figures given in the Dail (13.3.46, col 2315-6) indicate that of the 41,635 cottages provided in the 26 counties under loans sanctioned before 1922, 28,256 or almost 75% were in the twelve counties which are the focus of this study. Cork county took the biggest share of 7,509; Limerick next with 4,084; and Meath, 2,771. Thus by 1920 there was a concentration of cottages in the east Munster-Leinster area, housing workers who were permanent in the area and free from the fear of eviction. It is more than a coincidence then that the waves of trade union agitation which led to bitter conflict between farmers and workers during 1919-1923 and 1946-1948 were predominantly in that region.

The size of farms on which labourers worked would also have a bearing on any possible consciousness of difference between farmer and worker. The 1946 Census was the first to indicate the size of holdings which employed hired labour. It showed that only 24,500 from a total of 113,812 employees worked on farms under 50 acres, and 46,500 worked on the biggest units of over 100 acres (see third interim report, p.2-4, 8).

The type of farming pursued within the Dundalk–Limerick city–Bandon region was not a determining factor for the number of labourers in a district. Four principal types of farming were pursued in peace-time after 1900. During, and immediately after, the World Wars compulsory tillage changed the pattern slightly. Those outlying parts of Co. Dublin not involved in market gardening comprised, along with Kildare and Meath, the "grazing and fattening country with some highly specialized large farms" (T.W. Freeman, **Ireland: Its physical, historical, social and economic geography**, p.189,193). The biggest belt of land which encompassed Mid Cork and North Cork, East Limerick, South Tipperary and Kilkenny was devoted predominantly to dairying.

In County Wexford and North Tipperary "mixed farming with considerable tillage" was the norm (ibid.), while in East Cork, Waterford and East Wicklow mixed farming with stock raising and feeding for the store trade cattle predominated. No significant variation in patterns of labourer employment emerges with the type of farming, through the grazing and fattening country of Meath, Kildare and Dublin was the only region by 1946 to employ 1500$^+$ employees by 1,000 farmers.

Turning to other demographic features it is noted that females constituted an insignificant proportion in 1926 and following years in both the 'living in' and 'living out' sub-categories. They never comprised more than 2% in any province after 1926. The number living out fell from 846 in 1926 to 635 twenty years later and 264 in 1951. Similarly, the number living in fell from 402 in 1926 to 178 twenty years later and 99 in 1951.*

In 1926, 36,131 or approximately two out of every seven farm employees lived in. The proportion was not uniform at county level, however. In Leinster, apart from Kilkenny, not more than one in five lived in. Meath and Dublin were the extreme cases with only one in nine and one in ten living in respectively (ibid., 1926, Vol V, p.14-5). In Munster, Connacht and the three Ulster counties, on the other hand, the proportion living in averaged 33%, higher than the national figure (ibid.).

The number living in had fallen by 3,231 in 1936 and a further 6,472 in 1946, indicating a 25% decline over the twenty year period. This was reflected on a county basis, with eleven counties showing a decrease within 7% either way of the national average (ibid., 1946, Vol V, p.160-73). By 1966 only 5,332 employees living in remained. (James Deeny: **The Irish Worker: A Demographic study of the labour force in Ireland**, p. 28-29.)

The number of farm labourers living out showed a relatively small decrease 1926-1946, but then declined sharply between 1946 and 1951. The 1926 figure of 89,841 was down to 66,487 by 1951, and in 1966 the number was down to 21,848, when the 9,115 identified as unemployed farm labourers are excluded (see 1926 Census, Vol V, p.14-15; 1951 Census, Vol III, Part 1, Table 4, p.32-3; Deeny, p.28-29).

By 1960 the age distribution of farm employees also bore testimony to decline. By 1966 the 5,332 living in who remained were an ageing group since 42% were over 50 years, 21% were over 60 and only 28% were under 30 years. Similarly, with those living out, 35% were over 50 years in 1966, while 30% were under 30 (see Deeny, p.28-9).

With regard to conjugal status, the number of married among those living in was very low and declining as the century advanced. This was to be expected since it would be difficult for an entire family to live in, while a married employee would be unlikely to live apart from his family for the six-month or longer period required in the living in contract. The figure of 94% single in 1926 had increased to 95.6% in 1951 (see 1926 Census, Vol V, Table 4a, p.10; 1946 and 1951 **Census General Report**, Table 32, p.51; 1951 Census, Table 4a, p.13).

The number of married farm employees living out declined from 39.4% in 1926 to 36.7% in 1951. The 35,188 living out in 1926 who were married had 76,704 dependant children (1926 Census, Vol IX, Table 4a, p.43). That was the highest average figure for dependant children in the agricultural sector, and was amongst the highest for all the occupational groups in the country. While

---

*(See 1926 Census, Vol V, p.14-5, 210-27; and 1946 Census, Vol V, p.16; 1951 Census, Vol V, Table 6c, p.108-9.)

the number of families had declined to 29,903 with 59,795 dependant children in 1946, the average number of dependants (2:0) remained the highest in the agricultural sector (1946 Census, Vol X, Table 4a, p.43).

In summary, it is noted that the proportion of labourers remained significant in twelve counties up to 1946. The number declined sharply thereafter and was most accentuated in the case of those living in. The number of farm employees who married declined continually, but those who did marry had a higher number of dependant children than most other heads of households in the twenty-six counties.

(ii) Diet

A comparison of the labourer's diet for the years 1854, 1923 and 1947 shows a gradual improvement in the quantity and quality of food to the point where, in 1947, it was adequate if monotonous.

In 1854 a detailed record was made of farm workers' diet by the parish priests for each parish in the Archdiocese of Cashel (cited in James O'Shea, **Priest, Politics and Society in Post famine Ireland**, p.121). Potatoes were the staple diet, with Indian meal substituted in times of scarcity. Milk and vegetables were also available in most parishes, but meat was seldom consumed, and in the great majority of cases there was rarely any difference between the Sunday and weekday meals. Furthermore, it was emphasised that even this meagre fare was often uncertain and at times of economic recession the labourers' plight became desperate.

A survey by the ITGWU of the rural labourer's expenditure in the Fermoy, Mallow, Mitchelstown and Charleville area of Co. Cork in the spring of 1923 indicates that meat was then included. The point which the survey stressed, however, was that the outlined budget amounted to 38/- when the agricultural wage in the area was about 35/- and falling quickly with the deepening recession in agriculture. It was also emphasised that the budget made "no provision for clothing, boots, beer, tobacco, insurance, trade union fees or holidays" (see **Voice of Labour**, 14.4.23, from which the table below is also taken).

Table 2. Weekly Budget For A Rural Labourer, Wife And Two Children, In North Cork, Spring, 1923		s.	d.
Bread, one 4lb. loaf per day		1.	0
Butter, 2lbs. per week		4.	4
Milk, per quart per day		2.	11
Tea, 1lb. per week		3.	8
Sugar, 6 lbs. per week		3.	9
Bacon, 2lbs. per week		3.	0
Beef, 6lbs. per week		8.	0
Coal 1 1/2 cwt. per week		5.	4 1/4
Vegetables per week		1.	0
Light & Sundries		2.	6
Rent & Rates		2.	6
TOTAL	£1	18.	0 1/4

The inclusion of coal may seem surprising for rural areas with a supply of wood, but coal was burned with the wood. No allowance is made either for produce from the garden of a labourer's cottage, though presumably that would be more relevant in late summer and autumn when most vegetables became available.

During 1946-1948 the *National Nutrition Survey* examined the dietary habits and state of nutrition of over 2,600 representative families. The six categories devised were as follows: families living in Dublin city; those in towns whose populations were 10,000 and over; those in towns under 10,000 people; families in the old congested districts; farming families both over and under 30 acres; and farm workers' families (see **National Nutrition Survey**, Vols I-VII).

One hundred and seventy seven labourers' families throughout all of the 26 counties were included. The results showed that the diet of farm worker families was "sufficient" overall. It was notably inferior to that of farmers, both over and under thirty acres, but superior to that of many families of the unemployed, and superior to that of a high percentage of widows and old age pensioners (ibid., part V, p.11; part VI, p.23).

In farm employees' families, the consumption of bread, potatoes, meat, milk, eggs, vegetables and fruit increased consistently as income increased, and decreased with almost equal consistency as the number of persons in the family increased, suggesting the size of the portion eaten had still to be checked for reasons of economy. Significantly, the Survey remarked that in the labourer's family the consumption of milk at 5.1 pints per head per week was low for a rural survey. It contrasted with 9.2 pints per head per week in farming families outside the congested districts, while in Dublin city the average consumption was 4.8 pints. The Survey also noted that "the consumption of vegetables, eggs, meat and potatoes were all significantly lower in the farm workers' families" than in all farming families (ibid., part V, p.11). Furthermore, among the school-going children for the rural social groupings, 67% of the labourer children were regarded as being in a good nutritional state, compared to 71% for farmers under thirty acres and 79% for girls, 76% for boys of farmers with over thirty acres. Most of the remaining children in *all* social groupings were described as in a "fair" nutritional state (ibid., part VII, p.15).

On the other hand, if height and weight are accepted as barometers of children's health, then there was little difference between the children of farmers and labourers. It was recorded that while there was a variation in the height and weight of school children according to social class in the towns, in rural areas the variation was less marked. Indeed, at some ages it was noted that the heights and weights of farm employee children were greater than those of the children of farmers (ibid., p.11).

The National Nutrition Survey is unsatisfactory with regard to the diet of those labourers who lived in. The report assumed that their dietary intake was "determined by that of the farming families with whom they lived" (ibid.,

Part V, p.5). But employees living in claimed in the 1940s, as in previous decades, that they were fed very badly in many cases. The Survey was not justified therefore in taking the opposite for granted. For instance, Paddy Roche of Mount Collins, Co. Limerick, spent ten years living in, before 1946, and he testified to Pat Feeley in 1978 that the food had been mostly very bad. "Watery potatoes, green cabbage and a mug of water often constituted dinner. Supper was bread and milk without butter. Around two o'clock there was tea and a few slices of bread." (See: Pat Feeley, **Servant boys & girls in Co. Limerick**, in *Old Limerick Journal*, i (Dec 1979), p.34.)

(iii) Working Conditions

The working conditions of those living in were particularly susceptible to abuse. Written sources, broadcast material, personal recollections, folklore, songs, and literature all testify to harshness of conditions for the servant boy and girl on many farms.* Most sources also emphasise that some farmers treated the servant fairly. But the fact that it was solely at the discretion of the employer, twenty four hours a day, as to whether he would be a benevolent or malevolent despot was in itself the problem.

Some labourers who lived in described themselves as slaves, and the position was not totally dissimilar. In Munster, the indoor man was referred to as the *"servant boy"* even when the 'boy' was in his sixties. In the southern United States the same term was used when referring to adult Negroes. The statement by a Limerick labourer to McNabb in 1960 — "We were slaves but in our own way we were happy" — is identical with the sentiments attributed to Negroes by Frazier in 1939. (Patrick McNabb, **Limerick Rural Survey**, Third Interim Report, p.11; E.F. Frazier, **Negro Family in the United States**, quoted in McNabb, p.11.)

Certainly, the notorious hiring fairs bore many of the hallmarks of slavery. These were common in parts of Munster, Leinster and Ulster up the 1930s. Feeley calculates that the Newcastle West hiring fair began about 1884 and continued until the late 1940s, while McNabb reports the last one remembered at Kilmallock as 1939 (see Peadar O'Donnell, **Adrigoole**, and McNabb and Feeley in the works cited). Big farmers came to the Limerick fairs from North Cork, East Kerry and all parts of Co. Limerick. Those for hire gathered in the market places from early morning on the fair day, usually at the beginning of spring. Farmers tested the muscles of those for hire, and scrutinized them closely for signs of illness or weakness. The examination struck some observers as similar to that performed on animals. Peadar O'Donnell, for instance, who worked as an organizer for the ITGWU in Ulster in

---

*See: **Voice of Labour** 25.5.1922; letter from a labourer in **Irish People** 20.3.48; broadcast material — **Folklands**, presented by Seamus O'Cathain, RTE, Radio I, 10.4.83, 4.3.84, 11.3.84; **Women Today** 14.4.82, presented by Phil Crotty, RTE Radio 1, songs — *The Galbally Farmer, The Rocks of Bawn*; Literature — Peadar O'Donnell, **Adrigoole**.

1918-20, had first-hand experience of Strabane Fair, and devoted a chapter of his novel **Adrigoole** to it. He portrays one farmer asking another his opinion of a boy he had previously,

"'A good riser?' Sam asked.
'He's no' by hissel', but whistle an' he's up smart as a dog'..." (p.55.)

Patrick Mac Gill was himself hired out at Strabane and relates his experiences in **Children of the Dead End**. He began with the lines:

"Since two can't gain in the bargain,
Then who shall bear the loss
When little children are auctioned
As slaves at the Market Cross?" (p.34.)

On the other hand, it is suggested that some servants got the better of the bargain by doing as little work as possible. Despite his tale of hardship, a recent recollection suggests that Mac Gill himself was one of these. Paddy Mac Alleer, born in 1901, worked for Joe Young, the same farmer who hired Mac Gill, a few years after Mac Gill had left. In an interview with Seamus O'Cathain, broadcast on 11 March 1984 ('Folklands'), Mac Alleer recalled the weight of local opinion as being that "Mac Gill was too smart for Joe Young". Similarly, folklore contains many tales of servant boys playing tricks on farmers, though whether these are the products of wishful thinking, in an attempt to ridicule the employer, or based on fact, is more difficult to assess. (For examples of these tales, 'Folklands', 10.4.83, 4.3.84, 11.3.84.)

What is a fact is that hours of work were not fixed until 1936, except for the emergency years, 1917-21. Days off for the indoor worker depended on the goodwill of his employer. He could be sacked for standing under a tree from a shower of rain. If he wished to leave he had to give a month's notice or the farmer could refuse to pay him. Paddy Roche remembers the wettings and the wet clothes. He was not allowed to sit at the employer's fire, and the only hope of drying out clothes was at some neighbouring labourer's cottage (see Feeley, p.34).

After 1936 the Agricultural Wages Board (AWB) related compulsory minimum rates of pay to a 54 hour week. Overtime rates were set down for any hours worked over 54, and for Sunday work. However, a loophole persisted in Co. Cork and some other areas whereby the hours of work of those employed under the one-year 'contract system' were not regulated. In 1948 Con Moynihan, Chairman of the Cork Branch of the Federation of Rural Workers (FRW) made strong representations to the Chairman of the AWB on this matter, following which Dan Desmond, TD, Secretary, Cork Branch, FRW, raised it in the Dail.* An investigation was undertaken by the inspectors of the AWB, with the result that by 1950 the 'contract system' was subject to the nine-hour day.

The very fact, however, that the 9 hour, 6 day week, was still legal in 1948 was a source of grievance among farm workers. The bitter strikes of 1946-

---

* Con Moynihan, Carrigrohane, Co. Cork, in an interview with D. Bradley, 23.3.82, and Dail Reports, Vol 110, col 1032, 4.5.48.

7 were fought principally on the issue of shorter working hours. Farm workers in Leinster and East Munster increasingly contrasted their conditions of employment with those in towns and in industry. By 1940 the average hours per week worked by males in all industries and services was 44 1/2, when it was 54 in agriculture. (See **Statistical Abstract**, 1946, Table 249, p.102; *Some Statistics of Wages and Hours of Work in 1937 and previous years*.)

Similarly, farm employees were excluded from the *Conditions of Employment Act, 1936*, and *Holidays Act, 1939*, which guaranteed, inter alia, a weekly half-holiday and six days' annual holidays with pay.

Their own rising expectations also made many farm labourers resentful at their exclusion from legislation applying to other employees. When the Labour Court was established under the *Industrial Relations Act, 1946* agricultural workers were specifically excluded from it except for Section VI, which made provision for the investigation of disputes in agriculture in special circumstances. Despite a continuous campaign by the FRW after 1946, there was no reform until the *1976 Industrial Relations Act* replaced the AWB with a Joint Labour Committee.

Similarly, the Joint Labour Committees which replaced Trade Boards under the *1946* Act had control over *conditions* of work and holidays in addition to rates of pay. Despite continuous agitation, the AWB was never given control over working conditions.

Farm employees failed to get the benefits of the National Wage Agreements emanating from the Employer–Labour Conference during the early 1970s. The Joint Secretaries of the Employer–Labour Conference felt compelled to warn the AWB in 1972 that it was the only recalcitrant wage-fixing body and was placing the whole concept of national collective bargaining in jeopardy:

> "If, for any reason, such a large and important section of employees as agricultural workers appeared to be unable to gain the full benefits of a National Pay Agreement, the whole concept of such agreement would be seriously undermined..." (Letter from Employer–Labour Conference to AWB, 11.9.1972, copy in possession of members of the AWB).

By 1974 the AWB had made five orders which failed to implement the National Agreement (see Chapter 6).

Farm workers also benefitted less than most other categories of employee from social welfare legislation. The *Unemployment Insurance Act, 1920* covered almost all industries except agriculture. Men received 15/-, women 12/- for fifteen, later twenty six, weeks under the Act. After 1921 these amounts were supplemented for married men by 5/- a week for a wife and 1/- a week for each child. When asked in the Dail in 1922, if, in view of the hardships of unemployment in agriculture, he had considered the necessity of extending the Unemployment Act to that area, the Minister for Industry and Commerce, Joseph McGrath, replied that it would not be possible. He claimed that the collection of contributions would be difficult, the prevention of abuse in administration troublesome, that farmers would be definitely opposed to it and labourers either hostile or indifferent. In addition, because so much employment in agriculture was of a temporary or casual nature, the claims to benefit would be high (reported in **Voice of Labour**, 29.9.1922). Unemployment insurance was eventually extended to farm employees at a lower rate of contribution under the *Social Welfare Act, 1952*.

In the meantime, they had also been included in the *Unemployment Assistance Act, 1933*. However, up to 1966, under Employment Period Orders, unemployed farm labourers without dependants, along with relatives assisting and farmers of over £4 valuation, could be excluded from the 'dole' at certain times of the year when temporary employment would be more plentiful in rural areas. Such an order was made each year 1935-47 for the months of July to October (**First Report** Department Of Social Welfare, 1947-9, p.17-8).

With regard to injury benefit, farm workers gained from the *Workman's Compensation Act, 1900* which granted 50% of wages in the event of injury at work, without the onus to prove the employer's negligence. This was a considerable boon, as hitherto many labourers had been pauperised by injuries (see D. Farley, **Social Insurance and Social Assistance in Ireland**, p.10).

Similarly, the *Old Age Pensions Act, 1909* answered the long-standing demand for a replacement of workhouse relief with a system of care for those gone beyond economic usefulness. The fact that farm labourers were included in the non-contributory scheme because they could not afford the 4^d contribution out of the 11/- to 14/- wage indicated their need for such care (ibid., p.16-24).

Farm employees also benefitted from the *National Insurance Act, 1911* which provided for sickness benefit. Initially, any worker whose full rate of remuneration was less than 1/6 per day paid nothing, and 1/2 per week if earning from 1/6 to 2/0 per day. The state paid 1^d per week in both of those cases and the employer made up the balance. It was estimated in 1912 that most farm workers would pay the lower rate or nothing (W. Dudley Edwards, **The National Insurance Act in Ireland**, *JSSISI*, xiii, part 92, p.572). However, by 1924, when farm employers were paying the flat rate of contribution, they had difficulty in keeping up payments. That can be gauged from a Dail Debate in 1924 when the Minister for Finance was asked to discontinue the application of the Act to farm labourers in view of the fact that it "was the opinion generally expressed by both workers and their employers" that they would prefer to get outside the provisions of the Act (Vol 7, col 5, 25.4.24). If farm workers wished to get outside the Act, the explanation is that they were willing to sacrifice long-term benefit for short-term relief, because the Irish Insurance Commissioners recorded that up to 1924 agricultural employees had drawn as much in benefits as other workers at the rate of 10/- for a man, 7/6 for a woman, per week up to 1920, rising to 15/- and 12/- respectively thereafter (ibid.).

(iv) Social Status

"It is not the work that would pinch you but class distinction" (McNabb, p.11). This statement by a Limerick farm worker in 1960 indicates how strongly inferior social status was felt. Distinction was most obvious in the case of labourers living in. They were frequently put at a separate table, given inferior food, different crockery and, in some cases, no cutlery. After the evening meal they were not encouraged to stay in the kitchen.

Labourers living out frequently experienced this type of distinction at a threshing. Five of ten Cork labourers interviewed by myself recalled that at meal times during threshing an appointed person stood at the door, directing farmers and members of their families into one room and workers into another. The exception was the *"puller"*. This was a labourer who got "tobacco" or some other inducement to force the pace of work. He was promoted to the top table.

From the farmers' viewpoint the lack of training and education among farm workers as the century advanced made it difficult to change the traditional perception of ascribed status.

A Co. Waterford farmer, in 1954, lamented the lack of training and specialized education for labourers and wrote that it was a pity that the man who could be trusted with anything on the farm got the same rate of pay "as the fellow who would fall into the wheelbarrow through either awkwardness or laziness, but who would be neither lazy nor awkward with the farmer's daughter if the opportunity arose." (**Waterford Plough and Furrow**, ii, No.2, summer 1954, p.14).

Labourers, on the other hand, resented being thought ignorant by farmers, since there was little or no cultural difference between them. The majority of both classes had little time for books or book learning. Almost every worker interviewed by Mc Nabb said, "The farmers think they are better than us but we were used to more than a lot of them." (McNabb, p.12).

Mc Nabb also noted in 1960 how the traditional class structure was revealed in ordinary day-to-day pursuits. At public meetings people took up positions in the hall according to rank, age and sex. In the first two rows of seats were to be found middle-aged people of the professional or business class and farmers of high standing. These were the spokesmen and answered for the whole community. While they were present it was difficult to get other members of the audience to participate in discussion. In the next few rows were seated adult members of the farming class, and behind them again wives and other female members of the labourers' families. In the last rows, or standing at the back of the hall, were the male workers. Mc Nabb's conclusion was that this illustrated in a striking way that, although the farm worker was in revolt against the traditional class attitudes, he did not feel strong enough to challenge them in public (ibid.).

By 1960, the farm worker's devaluation of his own occupation had gone so far that he was sometimes ashamed to classify himself as a farm labourer. He was opting out of rural society. During the 1960s, however, a perceptible change came in the ascribed status of farm employee, due principally to the fact that the large scale introduction of tractors and machinery implied that those who adapted to the change were now 'skilled' workers. Table 3 indicates the scale of introduction of tractors during the 1950s.

Table 3. The Introduction Of Tractors And Decline In Permanent Farm Employees 1951–60.

Year	Number Of Permanent Male Labourers	Number Of Tractors
1951	68,934	16,037
1954	61,937	26,678
1957	53,500	32,700
1960	50,626	43,631

From A Submission to the A.W.B. by the F.R.W. 3.5.62; copy in possession of members of the AWB, Source ITJ, 1951-1960

Regarding the change in status, it may be significant that the 'situations vacant' column in the **Cork Examiner** changed its eighty year old heading *Farm Labour* to *Farm Workers* between 1961 and 1965. The word 'labourer' tended to have connotations of toil and drudgery, whereas 'worker' was a common term in the industrial sector. Another possible indication of change in perception of status is noted from Hannan's research in the mid 1960s (**Rural Exodus**, p.291-2). Damian Hannan presented Cavan teenagers with a list of 61 occupations, asking them to tick off those jobs which they felt they would be letting down their family by choosing. He presented them in an ascending order of status according to his own opinion. He put the occupation of Co. Council road worker lowest on the scale (No. 1) and farm labourer at No. 2. The perceived order put the farm worker at No. 9, higher than the street sweeper, messenger boy, general unskilled labourer, council road worker, petrol pump attendant, caretaker, doorman or porter, and laundryman (ibid.).

(v) Housing

The housing of those living in has given rise to most comment. Written and oral sources, personal recollections, broadcast material, folklore songs and literature (see footnote on page 15) all testify that the sleeping quarters of the servant boy and girl up to the 1950s was frequently an outhouse, loft or stable. The stable was chosen in the belief that heat from the horses provided warmth during the night. However, the pounding of feet from the animals could make sleeping impossible. Fleas and vermin in the bed were reported to be another hindrance to the slumbers of the indoor employee. In winter, drying off after wettings in the field were a big problem for those not allowed to sit at the employer's fire.

Up to the late 1940s, thousands of labourers living-out still lived in "workman's houses" belonging to the employer, despite the progress which had been made in providing almost 63,000 labourers' cottages in the Twenty Six

Counties by 1945 (Dail Debates, Vol 99, col 2315-6, 13.3.46). The fact that 24,000 more cottages were built 1945-64 suggests the remaining requirements after World War II (Paul A. Pfretzschner, **The Dynamics of Irish Housing**).

The occupant of a workman's house was in a vulnerable position because he was a tenant at will, his contract of work being on a yearly basis. In the event of a dispute with his employer he could be threatened with eviction. Six men interviewed by myself in Co. Cork recall that up to 1950 the movement of labourer families from one farm to another with all their belongings was seen on 'Lady Day', 25th March.

Those living in a local authority cottage were more independent. The *1883 Labourers Act* was not the first to deal with the housing of rural workers, but it was a milestone in that responsibility for building was partly transferred from landlords and farmers to the Boards of Guardians. But progress under the 1883 Act and amending legislation 1885-1903 was limited because many farmers used their positions on the Board of Guardians to hold up schemes (J.S. Donnelly, jnr., **The Land and the People**, p.240-2). In addition, the procedure was extremely cumbersome by 1903, with no less than nineteen necessary steps from the initial representation to the District Council to the letting of the new cottages (Nicholas J. Synnott, **Housing of the Rural Population in Ireland**, *JSSISI*, ix, 1904). Thus, by 1905, there were only 17,411 cottages occupied though there were 250,000 agricultural and rural "general labourers" (Synnott: **Proposal for a New Labourers Bill**, *JSSISI*, xi, 1906) .

Bryce's *1906 Labourers Act* and Birrell's *1911 Labourers Act* made a big breakthrough by cutting the costs, delays and interference of vested interests, by making the Local Government Board the final court of appeal for objections, by cheapening transfer of property and by system building. Furthermore, the Local Government Board was given greater powers to take action where local authorities defaulted on schemes. Thus, a total of almost 42,000 cottages for the Twenty Six Counties, 54,000 for the island as a whole, were provided under funds sanctioned before 1922. Each had a half acre of land from 1883, increased from 1892 to one acre. The Local Government Board required a minimum of two bedrooms and a kitchen, and laid down certain structural rules which prevented a regression to the worst features of the old cabins. Perishable materials were replaced by brick or local stone and mortar, and slates were preferred to thatch, as they were more easily maintained (see P.J. Meghen, **Housing in Ireland**, and Dail Reports, Vol 99, col 2315-6, 13.3.46; J.W. Boyle, **A Marginal Figure: The Irish Rural Labourer**, in Clark & Donnelly (eds.), Irish Peasants, p.332-3). Some indication of structural strength was that statistics published in 1945 showed that practically every house built since 1883 was still occupied (Dail Debates, Vol 99, col 2317, 13.3.46). Rents were subsidised from the beginning. The mean was 1/- a week, with a variation according to the prosperity of the district and the quality of the cottage.

Tables 4(a) and 4(b) show the number of cottages occupied in twelve Munster and Leinster counties contrasted with the remaining counties of Eire in 1945.

Table 4 (a). No. Of Cottages In 12 Munster & Leinster Counties

County	Total No. Of Labourers' Cottages Occupied At 31.3.1945	Average Rental (Exclusive Of Rates) of Cottage Per Week	
		s.	d
Cork	9,068	1	3
Limerick	5,455	1	3
Tipperary N.R.	2,075	1	7
Tipperary S.R.	2,583	1	6
Waterford	2,125	1	6
Kilkenny	2,237	1	8
Wexford	3,618	1	4
Wicklow	2,656	1	10
Carlow	1,477	1	9
Kildare	3,141	2	3
Meath	3,987	1	2
Dublin	3,285	3	1
Louth	1,595	1	4
TOTAL	43,302		

Table 4 (b) No. Of Cottages In Other Counties

County	Total No. Of Labourers' Cottages Occupied At 31.4.1945	Average Rental (Exclusive Of Rates) Of Cottage Per Week	
		s.	d.
Cavan	1,249	1	2
Clare	1,616	1	4 1/2
Donegal	1,937	1	8
Galway	1,320	1	6
Kerry	2,143	1	1
Laois	1,984	1	9
Leitrim	561	1	11
Longford	1,163	1	3
Mayo	526	1	8
Monaghan	633	1	6
Offaly	2,088	1	10
Roscommon	1,001	1	7
Sligo	893	2	0
Westmeath	2,237	1	2
TOTAL	19,351		

Dail Reports, Vol 99, col 2317, 13.3.1946

Over two thirds of the total were built in the twelve counties which are the focus of this study. The congested districts, which had large numbers of small farmers in bad housing, did not benefit substantially under the Labourers' Acts.

A group of workers on Mr. Robinson's farm: he employs upward of fifteen all the year round.

From Irish Press, 16.9.1946

chapter two

Farm Labourer Organisations In Co. Cork Before 1919

Constant factors which inhibited the organisation of farm labourers before World War I in Ireland were rural unemployment, the numerical weakness of farm employees vis-a-vis farmers and the continuing emigration of labourers. Combined with those factors was lack of finance, confidence and organisational skills amongst the farm workers. This survey illustrates that, when the above problems had been overcome and a movement initiated, further obstacles loomed. These were the inability to stay clear of nationalist politics, the fact that the leadership of the new movements was not of the labouring class, and uncertainty as to aims and objectives. Yet the years 1870–1914 saw four attempts to organise the farm labourers of Cork, putting that county in the vanguard of such efforts in Ireland.

Following the relaxation of the laws against associations in 1868, the Kanturk Labourers' Club was founded in October 1869. Its first open air meeting on 24 October to discuss the "Rights of Labour" was attended by up to 2,000 people (Sean Daly, **Cork: A City In Crisis**, Vol 1, p.14-5). The impact of the club outside Cork was slight, but within the county it was associated with, if not exactly in control of, the tumult in June/July, 1870. General labour unrest in Cork city that included widespread strikes was followed by stoppages of the agricultural labourers in Liscarroll and Charleville in the north of the county and Ballinhassig in the south. The rural workers demanded higher wages, broke some mowing machines and threatened to break others (J.S. Donnelly Jr., **The Land and the people of Nineteenth Century Cork**, p.237; Daly, op. cit., p.129-33). Wage demands were not satisfied on that occasion, but labourer agitation continued. By 1872 Philip F. Johnson of the Kanturk Labourers' Club, aware of the growing strength and militancy of agricultural trade unionism in England, came to believe that collaboration with the National Agricultural Labourers' Union (NALU) would be beneficial. Joseph Arch and other NALU leaders were eager for such co-operation also, in order to control the migration of Irish workers to England for the harvest, and to prevent them being used as strike breakers by English farmers. Thus the Irish National Agricultural Labourers' Union (INALU) was set up as a branch of the parent NALU at a labour convention in Kanturk on 14/15 August, 1873 (P.L.R. Horn, **The National Agricultural Labourers Union In Ireland, 1873-9**, in *IHS*, xviii, No 67 (March 1971), p.340-2, 346; Donnelly, op. cit., p.237).

From the viewpoint of the present study, most noteworthy are the reasons for the failure of INALU, considering that by the end of 1874 it had all but disappeared. A major cause of its failure was the constraints imposed by lack of an independent political stance, the leaders of the INALU feeling it necessary to work with Butt's Home Government Association from the union's inception. Butt was made President of the INALU at its inauguration, with permission granted to him to direct the new movement's energy towards agitation in Parliament (Horn, p.346). But to this support for the Home Rule movement the English leaders of the NALU were either unenthusiastic or opposed and, when it became clear that the political question would not be kept out of the labourers' movement, the NALU terminated its Irish link (Donnelly, p.238, Horn, p.347).

Another reason for the failure of the INALU was that its leadership lacked the radicalism to countenance direct action. The realities of the situation, perhaps, with the farm workers themselves preoccupied with searching out subsistence, made non-working class leadership inevitable. Philip F. Johnson, for example, was the owner of the Egmont Arms Hotel in Kanturk and a small tenant farmer. The limits of his radicalism were indicated when, during the strike in Kanturk in 1870, he called on the bosses to grant an increase in wages, but then warned that "there was a social perturbation existing at present in the country which should not be inflated." Those present went on to resolve with Johnson "that this meeting be emphatic in its declaration that this request [for an increase] emanates from no spirit of socialism, but from an anxious desire to advance the general interests of the country" (**Cork Examiner** (CE), 30.6.1879; Daly, **Cork** etc, p.116).

A further weakness in that labourers' union — and one recurrent in farm worker organisations up to World War I — was an ambiguity about aims. They seemed unsure whether to devote all their efforts to the improvement of wages and working conditions or to agitate for land also. This reflected the mentality of a people who were a rural proletariat but also farmers without land.

A new labourers' movement entitled the Labour League was established at a convention held in Limerick in May, 1881. Philip F. Johnson of Kanturk was again the chief organiser, but like its predecessor, by October 1881, it had allowed itself to become entangled in the major force in national politics, this time the Land League (Donnelly, **The Land** etc. p.238). While the Labour League was gathering momentum during the summer and autumn of 1881, Co. Cork once more experienced a wave of farm strikes, though these were not formally part of the League campaign. The occurrence of the strikes, however, are a further demonstration of the foremost position of Cork agricultural labourers with regard to agitation during the 19th Century. These strikes lacked planning, but were successful in the short term as large crowds of labourers marched from farm to farm in several parts of the county, demanding concessions and taking away labourers from those who would not accede (**West Cork Eagle**, 23, 30.7.1881; CE, 28.7, 10.8.1881; Donnelly, p.238).

Unbound labourers obtained from 1/- to 2/- increase, so that their weekly earnings now ranged from 9/- to 12/-, while bound men secured up to 1/- extra. Indoor farm servants gained £1, bringing their seasonal earnings to the £9–£12 range (**W. Cork Eagle,** 30.7, 6.8.1881; CE, 21,23, 27.7.1881; Donnelly, p.238-9). Soon, however, the labourers' agitation in Co. Cork was channelled into the bitter land war between farmers and landlords.

Kanturk was also the origin of the third effort to organise farm labourers. P.J. Neilan established the Kanturk Trade and Labour Association in 1889 with the assistance of D.D. Sheehan among others (D.D. Sheehan, **Ireland since Parnell,** p.172). It spread to neighbouring districts and villages, taking the title Duhallow Trade and Labour Association (ibid.). Michael Davitt became involved then and presided at the foundation of the Democratic Trade and Labour Federation in Cork early in 1890, which aimed to advance labour interests throughout the country*. However, within a few months the Federation was in shambles, due principally to the Parnellite split. D.D. Sheehan lamented: "The workers are the most vehement and vital elements in the national life, and they took sides more violently than any other section of the population" (Sheehan, p.173).

Such an outcome was further testimony to the vulnerability of labourers' movements to outside political developments.

The final effort at organisation during the 19th Century was the Irish Land and Labour Association (ILLA). The development of that movement requires detailed examination because it was still in existence, though in splinters, after World War I, and played a role in the hectic 1918–20 period. The ILLA was founded at a labour convention in Limerick Junction on 15 August, 1894. J.J. O'Shee, a young Carrick-on-Suir solicitor, was its secretary, while Cork representatives included Cornelius Buckley of St. Mary's, later to be a county councillor for many years. D.D. Sheehan joined after a few years, on his return to Cork (ibid., p.174).

The objectives of the ILLA were improved housing, welfare and working conditions and access to land holdings for labourers. Its strategy was to develop political rather than trade union action. The leadership felt that direct representation was essential because the 1884 enfranchisement of the labourer had so far failed to solve the labourer's problems (FJ, 16, 30.8.1894; UI, 4.8., 1.9.1894). At local level, conservative elements and farming interests had severely restricted the implementation of the Labourers' Acts, which dealt with cottage-building, since the cost would have been on the rates. The potential in the 1898 Local Government Act was therefore immediately recognised by the labourers. They, Sheehan commented:

> "were no longer a people to be kicked and cuffed and ordered about by the shoneens and squireens of the district; they became a very worthy class indeed, to be courted and flattered at election times" (p.176).

*****United Ireland,** (UI), 25.5.1890; **Freeman's Journal,** (FJ), 22.1.1890; Arthur Mitchell, **Labour in Irish Politics,** 1890-1930; **The Irish Labour Movement in an Age of Revolution,** p.16.

Success in building up the organisation, however, was limited, and concentrated mostly in three counties — Cork, Limerick, and Tipperary. Table 5 indicates ILLA progress over its first six years.

Table 5.	
Year	Number of ILLA Branches
1899	66
1900	98
1901	98
1902	102
1903	102
1904	144
Reports of Annual Convention of the ILLA in Cork Examiner, 16.8.1899; 16.8.1900; 16.8.1901; 16.8.1902.	

Once more developments in nationalist politics dominated a labourers' movement. From the outset in 1894, Redmond, Dillon and William O'Brien considered the ILLA to be a dangerous deviation from the Party line (FJ, 16.8, 29.10, 26.11.1894; UI, 13.1, 5.2, 12.5.1894; Lyons, p.271). O'Brien's position here is particularly noteworthy, in view of his later deep involvement with the ILLA. To offset the potential threat, it suited the Irish Party leaders to admit the ILLA to the National Convention that re-united national politics in 1900. ILLA leaders, on the other hand, felt that alliance with the Party, while at the same time maintaining an independent identity, would be to their advantage. Differences surfaced almost immediately, however, when the death of Dr. Tanner caused a by-election in mid-Cork in 1901, a constituency recognised as having a high proportion of farm labourers as voters. When various manoeuvres failed, the Party was obliged to accept D.D. Sheehan, who won principally on the ILLA ticket.

Two years later, the in-fighting started that was to split the Party once more. That gave rise to the factionalism in Cork politics which was to divide and weaken the agricultural labourers' movement until the end of World War I. William O'Brien resigned from the Party in 1903, when his policy of "reconciliation" was rejected by Redmond. In 1905, "without a party and short temporarily of a policy" (J.V. O'Brien, **William O'Brien and the course of Irish Politics**, p.166), O'Brien took up the labourers' cause and spoke at ILLA meetings throughout counties Cork, Kerry, Limerick, Clare, Tipperary and Wexford.

Potential for agitation was great because, since the Wyndham Act had catered for the tenant farmers, legislation to provide for the labourers' needs was seen in many quarters to be the next most pressing issue. O'Brien's activity caused increasing worry to the Irish Party leaders. As the general election approached, Dillon's letters to Redmond stressed with increasing urgency the need to combat O'Brien's takeover of the ILLA (Lyons, **John Dillon**, p.287; Dillon to Redmond, 19,23,30.8.1905; 25.9.05; Redmond Papers; and O'Brien, p.167). Finally, on the eve of the election, the ILLA secretary, J.J. O'Shee, who was loyal to Redmond, disaffiliated dissident branches so that they could not be present at the conventions to choose candidates (**Cork Weekly News**, 21.10.1905; CE, 12.1.1906; **Irish People**, 7.10.1905, 27.1.1906, 3.2.1906).

Thus two rival land and labour associations emerged after the 1905 election. D.D. Sheehan had consolidated the original organisation in Co. Cork in the process of organising his own re-election. J.J. O'Shee, Kendal O'Brien and others, with party approval, led the other association in an effort to take support from Sheehan. Considerable confusion was generated for many branches which had no loyalty to personalities. "A plague on both your houses" might have been the attitude of the North Tipperary Divisional Council of the ILLA when, in August 1907, it passed a resolution not to affiliate to either Sheehan's or O'Shee's movement for the present (CE, 10.7.1907).

The in-fighting meant that the labourers' energies were being dissipated on issues that were of no relevance to the improvement of their living conditions. There was one concrete achievement, however, for which both Redmondites and O'Brienites were zealous in claiming credit. This was Bryce's *Labourers' Act, 1906* which, along with Birrell's *Labourers' Act, 1911*, greatly assisted cottage building. Co. Cork had 7,509 cottages, or 14% of the total for the 32 counties by 1922.

The passage of the 1906 Act helped in the short term to counter-act the demoralization caused by the split, because each local branch had a role to play in drawing up lists of those entitled to cottages and promoting the cases of applicants. Such leverage could be used as a stick as well as a carrot by the branch. Thus we find Carrigrohanebeg branch, near Ballincollig, threatening that those members in arrears would not be listed at the enquiry for cottages (CE, 13.1.1906).

In the long term, however, the split seriously weakened the labourers' cause. O'Shee's Irish Land and Labour Association and Sheehan's County Cork LLA held separate annual conventions 1907–1909. There was continuous dialogue concerning re-unification, which left little time for much else. By August, 1908 the stumbling block was the chairmanship of a reunited association. O'Shee insisted that Sheehan would have to go, while the mid-Cork MP pleaded that for him his position was a matter of principle, not personality. The situation became more complicated with the advent of the first 1910 general election. Sheehan's association split in two on the eve of the election, thus giving three Land and Labour Associations from 1910 until 1915.

This split was precipitated by Sheehan's assumption that the Cork County LLA would be part of his election machinery. Others on the Cork Co. Committee of the Association, notably Patrick J. Bradley, MCC, of Bishopstown, chairman of the Co. Committee, were anxious for moves towards reunification with O'Shee. Thus, when a "special convention" of the Cork County Committee was advertised for New Year's Day, 1910, Bradley put a notice in the **Examiner** denouncing the meeting as it "has been called for political motives, and without consulting the Co. Committee" (CE, 1.1.1910). The degree of passion aroused among the labourers is indicated by the exchange of punches at the "convention". When D.D. Sheehan, surrounded by a party of labourers, was approaching the entrance to the Municipal Buildings, he was met by another group, "who cheered for Mr. P.J. Bradley, MCC." Some conflict of a minor character took place at the door leading to the Council Chamber, and a few blows were exchanged. There were shouts of "put them out" and "down with them" from Mr. Sheehan's supporters, and a rush was made on the body of interrupters who were hustled towards the door, but they repelled the rush on them, and again returned cheering for Messrs. Bradley and Hayes. "Both parties swayed in a noisy fashion for some time in the passage outside the Chamber proper and eventually the body supporting Sheehan and Buckley succeeded in ejecting their opponents" (CE, 3.1.1910).

Such an occurrence was not, admittedly, unique in the factionalism of Cork politics at the time, but it does highlight the fact that rather than building solidarity among the labourers, the ILLA had actually done the opposite. The bitterness continued to manifest itself during 1910, with allegations that houses were attacked in broad daylight, while in one case in Lehenagh, a man was called a "Molly Maguire" and stones were thrown at his house while he himself was working in his garden! (CE, 16.8.1910.)

Bradley proceeded after 1910 to build a private empire under the title, Cork City and County Land and Labour Asscociation, catering for those in the hinterland of the city and in East Cork, but also attempting to poach branches from the Sheehan stronghold of mid-Cork (see, for example, CE, 18.3.1911). After the introduction of national insurance with the 1911 Act, Bradley also built up the Land and Labour Approved Society which had assets of over £20,000 by 1919 (AGM of Land & Labour Approved Society, reported in CE, 17.7.1919). In addition to agricultural labourers, that society catered for dockers and general labourers. Meanwhile, William O'Brien formed the All-for-Ireland League on 31 March, 1910, establishing very close ties with Sheehan's LLA. A study of the 24 All-for-Ireland branches that existed by 14 May, 1910 reveals that "even those few outposts were equally adopted to membership in the older LLA — at least the same place names appear in the listings" (O'Brien, p.198). Thus personalities and issues not central to the problems of the labourer continued to dominate his efforts at organisation up to World War I.

It would, on the other hand, be simplistic to attribute all the ILLA shortcomings to political manipulation by nationalist leaders. The constant factors of unemployment, emigration and consequent diminishing numerical strength weakened the Association (see Chapter 1).

A further weakness of the ILLA was that it never succeeded in mobilising to the full whatever labourer potential did exist. Actual numbers in individual branches or in the overall association were never mentioned, creating the suspicion that they were not great. Most local secretaries were skillful enough at propaganda, however. The constant stream of reports on branch meetings in the newspapers spoke of "large attendances" and "splendid gatherings".

There is evidence too that all labourers did not identify their interests exclusively with the LLA. For example, a vacancy arose on Cork County Council for the Ballincollig Division in July, 1906. A joint convention of the United Irish League and LLA was held at Ballincollig on 15 July, 1906 to choose a candidate. Both sides put forward a Rural District Councillor for the position. The LLA candidate, Timothy Forde of Carrigrohanebeg, lost, and then complained bitterly of ingratitude on the part of some members of his own association who voted against him.

> "He was ashamed that any body of men... should forget their principles and vote against one of their own members and nominee" (CE, 16.7.1906).

Indeed, at times farmers were welcomed into the LLA. Thus, for example, at the Castlemagner, North Cork LLA meeting on 17 January, 1906, the chairman said: "...he was proud to see such a large number of farmers present, which proved their branch in no way antagonistic to the [United] Irish League" (CE, 17.1.1906).

Reading through the branch reports in the press, one also senses that after the first decade a certain smugness existed in the association. Names of those who attended regularly and their utterances are listed in great detail, giving the impression of a correlation between attendance and desire to see one's name in the newspaper. The same names dominate branches from year to year, suggesting that the more "respectable labourers", those who had got cottages in the first wave of building before 1906, were mainly involved. That position is further suggested by the reaction of the politicians, normally good barometers of grassroots opinion. By 1908 William O'Brien felt secure enough to specify to an LLA audience that bigger holdings should be provided only for "particularly meritorious labourers". Thirty out of every hundred acres of untenanted lands should, he said, be set apart yearly by way of premiums in the different unions to such labourers as may be found to have managed their present plots to the best advantage. There would thus be opened the prospect of a higher career in life for labourers who would have deserved it by lives of sobriety, industry and intelligence (CE, 12.8.1908).

D.D. Sheehan spoke at the same meeting, endorsing O'Brien's view, the implication of which was that the majority of labourers who had not yet received cottages would have to prove themselves in such a holding sometime in the future before being given the opportunity of a bigger tenancy.

Finally, structural weaknesses in the ILLA contributed to its problems. Power rested in the hands of a few top officials, thus inviting abuse and self-perpetuating committees. Four of the twelve-man Central Council were co-opted annually (CE, 16.8.1899). O'Shee, Sheehan and Bradley all consolidated their top positions once they achieved them and treated their associations as personal property. Their positions allowed them to waste the energy of the movement on factionalism, obscuring the very basic question of whether the LLAs were aiming primarily for tenant status for the labourers or concentrating on improving their position as wage earners. In the final analysis, the very strategy of faith in political activity and alliance with the Irish Party was open to question. Direct action through trade unionism was an alternative strategy, the advent of which among farm workers in Co. Cork on a serious scale must now be examined. The consequent interaction of trade unionism with the LLAs will be an interwoven theme.

(ii) The Growth Of The ITGWU And Interaction With The LLA In Co. Cork, 1917–1918.

Trade unionism became successful among farm labourers in the years after 1917 because the Great War transformed the economic parameters governing the operation of the labour market. Shortage of manpower replaced chronic pre-War unemployment, thereby increasing the labourer's sense of security, while the growing demand for foodstuff enhanced his position when demanding an improvement in conditions. Trade union growth remained insignificant for the first two years of the War for numerous reasons. Initial awe at the momentous events occurring in Europe, along with pleas for unity, had some effect. Separation allowances and regular wages were a novelty for a time for many working class families. Then, too, it took time for the labourers to become conscious of how circumstances had altered in their favour and that agriculture was becoming increasingly prosperous.

Furthermore, the trade union movement itself had to recover from the setbacks of 1913 before it could tackle the problem of expansion into the countryside. The Lock-out had left a deep scar, so that workers were reluctant to combine or strike for better conditions despite the improved economic position (David Fitzpatrick, **Strikes in Ireland, 1914-21**, in *Saothar vi*, p.28). Military recruitment disrupted unions, especially those like the ITGWU which catered for unskilled workers. Thus, in May 1915, William Partridge admitted to a Cork audience that no less than 2,700 former ITGWU members were in the trenches, at a time when current membership was less than 5,000 (ibid.). The disorganisation of the ITGWU became even worse after the 1916 Rising because of the execution or imprisonment of many organisers and the destruction of Liberty Hall. Then by increasing political divisions in the county, the Rising made union organisation more difficult.

As was to be expected the political masters of the Land and Labour Associations were more concerned with the War effort than the grievances of the labourers. J.J. O'Shee recruited for the army in Ireland (see, for example, CE 19.8.1915), while D.D. Sheehan carried out several recruiting campaigns and then served in France himself (CE, 30.7.1919). There was mounting frustration among ordinary members of the association by the beginning of 1917, but yet confusion about the steps required to advance their position.

A meeting of the Queenstown (Cobh) branch in January 1917 demonstrates this. Mr. Downing, speaking on the question of affiliation, said he favoured joining with Mr. O'Shee (ILLA) rather than the Cork City and County LLA (Bradley) because O'Shee was more powerful, had the Irish Party behind him, and did great work, while no practical results had been achieved by the other association. Mr. O'Neill countered by demanding that they should not join the Irish Party or any party but join a trade union (CE, 24.1.17). Patrick Bradley then addressed the meeting, describing himself as "the paid servant of the working men of the city and county". That referred to his income from affiliation fees to the LLA, plus that derived from the secretaryship of the Land and Labour Approved Society. His strategy now, Bradley said, was to call on all LLA branches to demand 25/- per week, some labourers at that date earning only 9/- (ibid.). There, at last, was the aim, if not the means, of pushing the wage issue, though the meeting showed that many members were still pre-occupied with other questions, such as that of housing improvements by means of political influence.

Labourer agitation in Co. Cork became more proletarian in emphasis by the week from January onwards, however. On St. Patrick's Day about 50 labourers of the Churchtown Labour League in North Cork went on strike and conducted protest marches en route from Buttevant to Charleville demanding "fifteen shillings a week plus diet" (C.D. Greaves, **The Irish Transport and General Workers Union:** The Formative Years 1909-23, p.179).

The pattern of ILLA activity in other counties at the beginning of 1917 reflects a similar divergence of objectives to that found in Cork. Local factors had a significant influence. Thus, in Clare, where the predominance of the small farmer mentality rubbed off on the labourers, the latter continued to demand a share in the land distribution (David Fitzpatrick, **Politics and Irish Life 1913-21:** Provincial Experience Of War And Revolution, p.244) In North Kerry, similarly, the issue of land division came to the fore. On 10 March, 1917 about 130 labourers marched into Tralee three abreast to protest against the sale of a large farm at Ardfert (Greaves, p.179).

A meeting of the LLAs in counties Laois and Carlow on 4 February, 1917, on the other hand, reflected the Queenstown position. The meeting considered "reorgnisation along trade union lines". Rent and allotments were also discussed, but the emphasis was on the demand for a wage of 25/- a week (ibid.).

The establishment of the Agricultural Wages Board (AWB) and a minimum rate of pay in September, 1917 had therefore a very significant impact on the LLAs. It gave a state licence and support for wage demands, thereby pointing out the direction in which the Association's energies must be expended in the immediate future. The credibility of the various strands of LLA was enhanced as three of the six worker representatives on the AWB for all of Ireland were drawn from their ranks. The appearance of those three names side by side in Department of Agriculture bulletins gave no hint of former factionalism. Timothy Raleigh, Pallasgreen, Co. Limerick, represented O'Shee's movement; Cornelius Buckley, MCC of Fair Hill, Cork, had been a D.D. Sheehan supporter to the end. But most ironical of all was the fact that the Department of Agriculture erroneously conferred the title "President, *Irish Land and Labour Association*" on the other Cork member of the Board, none other than Patrick J. Bradley (see, for example, DAT II, xviii, No. 3, April 1918, p.308).

It was the government announcement of the setting up of the AWB that also gave the ITGWU the final spur to cater seriously for farm workers. The union leadership would not admit that, and indeed, they proceeded to denigrate the Board within a year of its establishment. But the role of the AWB in giving the union a foothold in the countryside cannot be underestimated. Compelling an employer to carry out his legal obligations was a new motive for trade union organisation on the farm, and even reluctant rural workers could no longer see such organisation as a conspiracy against the state. Also important, from the union viewpoint, was the knowledge that a guaranteed wage would enable farm labourers to keep up their subscriptions. The government announcement of its decision to establish the AWB came on 9 March, 1917. It was hardly a coincidence that, on 21st March, Acting General Secretary, Thomas Foran, proposed to the committee of No. 1 Branch, ITGWU the objective of "getting all the agricultural workers of Ireland organised" (Greaves, p.180). He argued that, if their standard of living on the farms could be raised sufficiently, the labourers would not wish to come into the towns and compete in the streets.

The Transport Union did, of course, have some earlier limited experience of organising farm workers. Jim Larkin began to recruit them in June, 1913, campaigning mostly on Sundays in and around the villages of Baldoyle, Kinsealy, Swords, Finglas and Lucan. A relatively detached historian writes in these terms on what Larkin found there:

> "the harshness and misery of the agricultural labourer's lot rivalled in intensity the worst experiences of his inner-city colleague" (Dermot Keogh, **The Rise Of The Irish Working Class, The Dublin Trade Union Movement and Labour Leadership 1890-1914**, p.183).

As the harvest approached in August, Larkin threatened a strike. The Farmers' Association, with no room to manoeuvre, signed an agreement on 17 August giving increases of up to 20% on labourers' wages. The hours of work agreed were from 7 am to 6 pm in winter with one meal hour, and 6 am to 6 pm in summer with two meal hours. Casual labour was paid at 4/- a day and 5/- a day up to 1 November. While the new conditions were far from satisfactory, they did give the labourer a contract for the first time in his life (**Irish Worker**, 19, 26.7.1914; Keogh, p.183; Greaves, p.89-90; Emmet Larkin, **James Larkin** Irish Labour Leader 1876-1947, p.104-5). Many employers, however, only awaited the opportunity to break the contracts, and in November, when Larkin was busy elsewhere, men were discharged who would not sign the 'document' stipulating that they leave the Transport Union. At Swords sixteen possession orders to remove recalcitrant labourers from their cottages were granted in a single day (Greaves, p.118).

The Transport Union continued to cater for farm labourers after the Lockout but the numbers were not significant before 1917. At the end of 1915, Dublin No. 1 Branch, which had the bulk of total union membership, recorded only 63 agricultural labourers from a branch membership of 3,659 (ibid., p.152-3).

Before dealing with the rivalry between the ITGWU and LLAs it is appropriate to consider the other theme associated with the spectacular expansion of the Transport Union into the countryside. This refers to the favourable impression on farm workers created by the success of the newly formed branch of the ITGWU in the local town. The link thus formed between town and country workers was of vital importance. In the past, the only districts where trade unionism had taken root in rural Ireland were those such as Kanturk where there was a large concentration of labourers. But since, for Ireland as a whole, farm labourers were only about 20% of the agricultural workforce, long term success through trade unionism would be greatly assisted by alliance with the town workers. Such a combination would offset the numerical disadvantage and sense of isolation in the countryside, while the knowledge that a trade union with a proven track record would back them would stiffen the courage of the farm workers.

As in 1913, the first advances into the countryside were made in the villages of Co. Dublin. On 11.3.17, Thomas Foran, William O'Brien (not to be confused with the William O'Brien of the Home Rule Party) and Thomas Lawlor addressed farm workers at Blanchardstown and succeeded in forming a branch that day (ibid., p.18). Lawlor then proceeded to organise Rathcoole, Clondalkin and Baldoyle.

Outside of Dublin, the ITGWU made most rapid advances in Cork City. Denis Houston, who proved a very effective organiser, started work in Cork in October 1916. Tadg Barry, who was to lead the farm workers of the county in the strikes campaigns of 1919 and 1920, was associated with Houston from the beginning, speaking for example at the meeting held by Houston at Cork City Hall 21 November, 1916. Houston took the builders' labourers of the city out on strike at the beginning of April, 1917, work being resumed a week later pending arbitration by the Director of Munitions. By the start of May, Houston had set up six branches in Cork City and had won increases for workers in the coal trade, the grist mills and two shipping lines (ibid., p.184). The push into the countryside followed, with the Blarney branch being founded on 23 June, 1917. The increasing workload for the organiser is indicated by the fact that Cathal O'Shannon was appointed Houston's assistant in mid-July 1917, while the leasing of the spacious Connolly Hall on Camden Quay in August is further evidence of a healthy state of affairs.

By the beginning of 1918 then, the Transport Union clearly had a good Cork base from which to make an appeal to the farm workers. It did not achieve immediate success as it had done in Co. Dublin, the reason being the fierce opposition of the Land and Labour Associations. Before charting that opposition in Co. Cork in detail, it is valuable to examine the pattern of resistance from the older labourer organisations, to the concept of the One Big Union (OBU) in other parts of the country.

In counties where the older organisations were long established, opposition lasted until 1920. Elsewhere initial suspicion and resistance were overcome relatively quickly, as had occurred in Co. Dublin. Thus in Co. Waterford, where the LLA had never been strong because Parnellite sentiment mistrusted the anti-Parnellite ILLA, those Land and Labour branches that did exist were quickly absorbed into the ITGWU*. In January, 1918 the Meath Labour Union resolved to affiliate to the ITUC, a step nearer the ITGWU, but when they read shortly afterwards of the support expressed for the Russian Revolution at ITUC meetings in Dublin, they concluded that the Irish Trade Union movement was heavily infected with socialism. They therefore reversed their decision on 2 April, intending instead to affiliate to a proposed new organisation styled "The Association of Rural Workers and Workmen's Labour Unions" (Greaves, p.192-3). The Johnstownbridge, Co. Kildare branch of the ILLA declared its intention of establishing a "Labour Union" for the whole county in opposition to the Transport Union (ibid.). Similarly in Co. Clare, new branches of the ILLA were set up in 1917 and 1918, and it was not until July, 1919 that the ITGWU absorbed the LLA in Clare. Even then, meetings of LLA branches in the county are noted after that date (Fitzpatrick, **Politics & Irish Life**, p.243-4).

At the beginning of 1919 the Executive Committee of the Transport Union intensified its efforts to win over the LLA in more counties. On 2 February, Thomas Foran agreed on the principle of amalgamation with LLA leaders in Co. Laois, the result being that LLA branches in Ballybrittas, Castletown, Borris-in-Ossory, Mountrath and Mountmellick fused with the ITGWU. Attention was then paid to Co. Wexford, the stronghold of the Irish National Trade and Labour League, the President of which, James Murphy, was on the AWB. The "Bunclody agreement" which followed safeguarded the national insurance contributions of Trade and Labour members, so that 8 branches in the county amalgamated with the Transport Union during 1919 (Greaves, p.245). Yet the opposition of other branches in Wexford continued throughout 1920, and the ITGWU admitted in September 1920: "Owing to the previous attachment of a large number of men to weak local unions, it is only recently that the OBU [One Big Union] has got properly going in the county... Even yet, the organisation is not by any means what it should be" (**Watchword of Labour**, 18.9.1920).

---

*Emmet O'Connor, UCG MA Thesis, **The Politics of the Labour Movement in Waterford since 1890**; Emmet O'Connor, **Agrarian Unrest and the Labour Movement in County Waterford 1917-23**, in *Saothar vi*, p.40.

As might be expected from the fact that Cork had been the traditional stronghold of the LLAs, the pattern in that county was one of outright opposition to the ITGWU from the two surviving factions of the Association until September 1918, and resistance until 1920 in the case of Bradley's organisation. But Bradley and Cornelius Buckley capitalized on their prestige as members of the central AWB to strengthen existing branches and start new ones. Their main function now was to compel farmers to pay the AWB rate, and where necessary to take steps to recoup arrears. The LLAs could compete favourably with the ITGWU at that task, since they had the advantage of being long established.

The AWB rates which came into effect on 10.11.17 gave 25/- per 60 hour week in Group 1 areas, 22/6 for Group II and 20/- for those in Group III districts. Group I comprised mostly of Co. Boroughs and Urban Districts, Group II areas adjacent to smaller towns, and Group III more remote districts and most parts of the western counties. By the end of November 1917 Patrick Bradley's Association had mustered 14 branches from within a ten-mile radius of the city in addition to the Queenstown branch (CE, 20.11.17). The old divisions in the Land and Labour ranks were then resurrected when Bradley put a notice in the **Examiner** warning branches that a meeting called for 25.11.17 was not under the auspices of his Association (CE, 24.11.17). It was, obviously, called by Cornelius Buckley and the ILLA. Twelve parishes attended this meeting and six of them — Ballincollig, Blarney, Whitechurch, Bishopstown, Little Island and St. Mary's — had been represented (though by different people) at the opposition's gathering the previous week (CE, 26.11.17). (See Map on Pages 38-9.) Constant campaigning brought Bradley's representation to 21 branches at a 1918 New Year's "Convention", while 18 branches sent delegates to the ILLA meeting the following weekend (See CE, 27.11.1917; 8, 11, 15, 18, 23.12.1917; 1, 2, 8.1.1918).

By February 1918, the agricultural section of the ITGWU was recruiting in Bishopstown (CE, 12.2.1918), which meant that three organisations were by then competing for the support of the labourers in that parish. The Transport Union took the offensive. This was Patrick Bradley's home branch and parish, and the ITGWU immediately attacked his status as a member of the AWB. On 15.2.18 the Bishopstown section of the ITGWU passed a resolution "looking on the Wages Board as a farce and a complete failure" (CE, 15.2.18). By 7.3.18 the Transport Union had three agricultural branches at Whitechurch, Ballincollig and Upper Glanmire, in addition to the Bishopstown section.

The aggressive posture was continued when that union attempted to dictate terms that its members would accept for the coming year when the contracts of bound men came up for renewal on the traditional 'Lady Day', 25 March. Labourers in those four parishes were 'ordered' not to bind themselves until they saw the scale of wages agreed upon (CE, 7.3.18). An expensive quarter-column advertisement was then placed in the **Cork Examiner** stating the terms that "the organised agricultural labourers" in those parishes would accept. Demands included 30/- per week without board, lodgings and perquisites, 5/- above the AWB rate. Hours were to be from 6 am to 6 pm in summer, 6 am to dark in winter, while 2/6 was demanded for Sunday work. These demands are significant in that the ITGWU were demonstrating to labourers and farmers alike all over the county that they intended to impose their own terms in the future (CE, 9.3.18).

In contrast, the ILLA in Cork County was now showing weakness and hesitation. On St. Patrick's Day, at a meeting of the Co. Cork organising committee, Mr. Walsh of Youghal said that his branch consisted of approximately 300 members. He found that the ILLA was more for the benefit of agricultural labourers than town labour, "and what he would like to know was if they could form, under the ILLA, a trades union to benefit town workers only". Cornelius Buckley suggested that a special meeting of the Central Executive should be called for the purpose of considering the matter. While such deliberations were taking place, the ITGWU stepped in and seized the opportunity. The Youghal workers affiliated to that union in April, 1918, with the above-mentioned Mr. Walsh becoming branch secretary (CE, 18.3.18).

The lack of initiative in the ILLA was further demonstrated on 7 April. Florence O'Sullivan, RDC county organiser, reported that he had received a number of communications from South Cork, where the labourers expressed a wish to be organised and "whilst they in that association were anxious to tap every district in the county, he was afraid the restrictions on train facilities would hamper their operations a good deal" (CE, 8.4.18). The efforts of the branches did not inspire great confidence either. In mid-April a Kilmichael labourer, a member of the ILLA, went into dispute with his employer. The branch decision to pay him £1 a week *"while possible"* (CE, 15.4.18) did not convey the impression of a big strike fund.

After a few more months of soul-searching and rhetoric the Cork Executive of ILLA decided that its best interests could be served by joining the ITGWU. One of the earliest indications of the new policy was at a meeting of the South Kilmurry ILLA branch in mid-September, where a letter was read from F. O'Sullivan RDC county organiser, urging the branch to join up with the ITGWU (13.9.18). With that bastion of resistance taken, the Transport Union made evident progress, Houston bringing the farm labourers in the significant centres of Fermoy and Macroom into the union by the beginning of October (CE, 19.9.18; 2.10.18).

The census of membership taken by the ITGWU on 30 June, 1918 gives further evidence of the part played by Land and Labour resistance in retarding the recruitment of farm labourers.

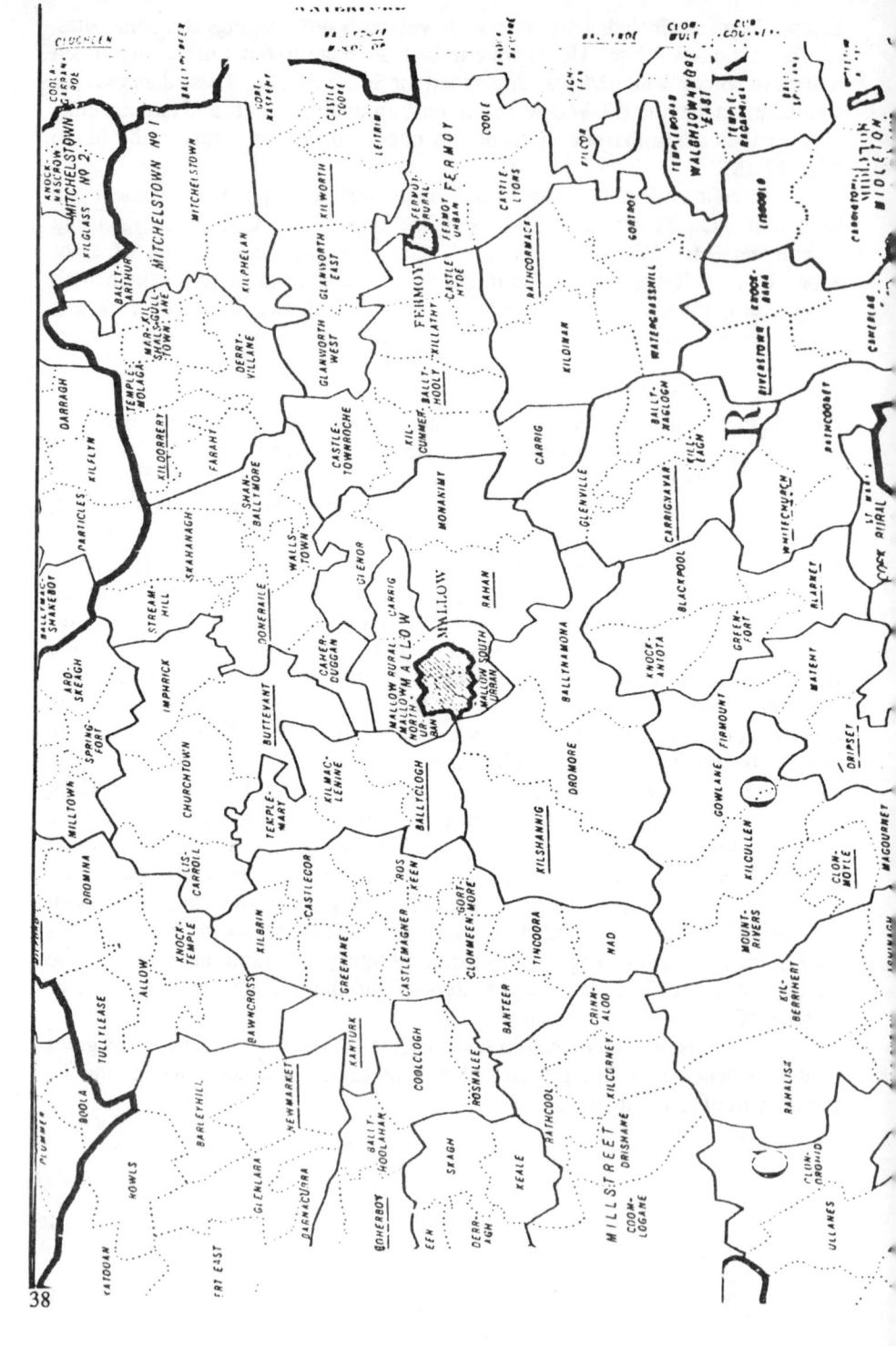

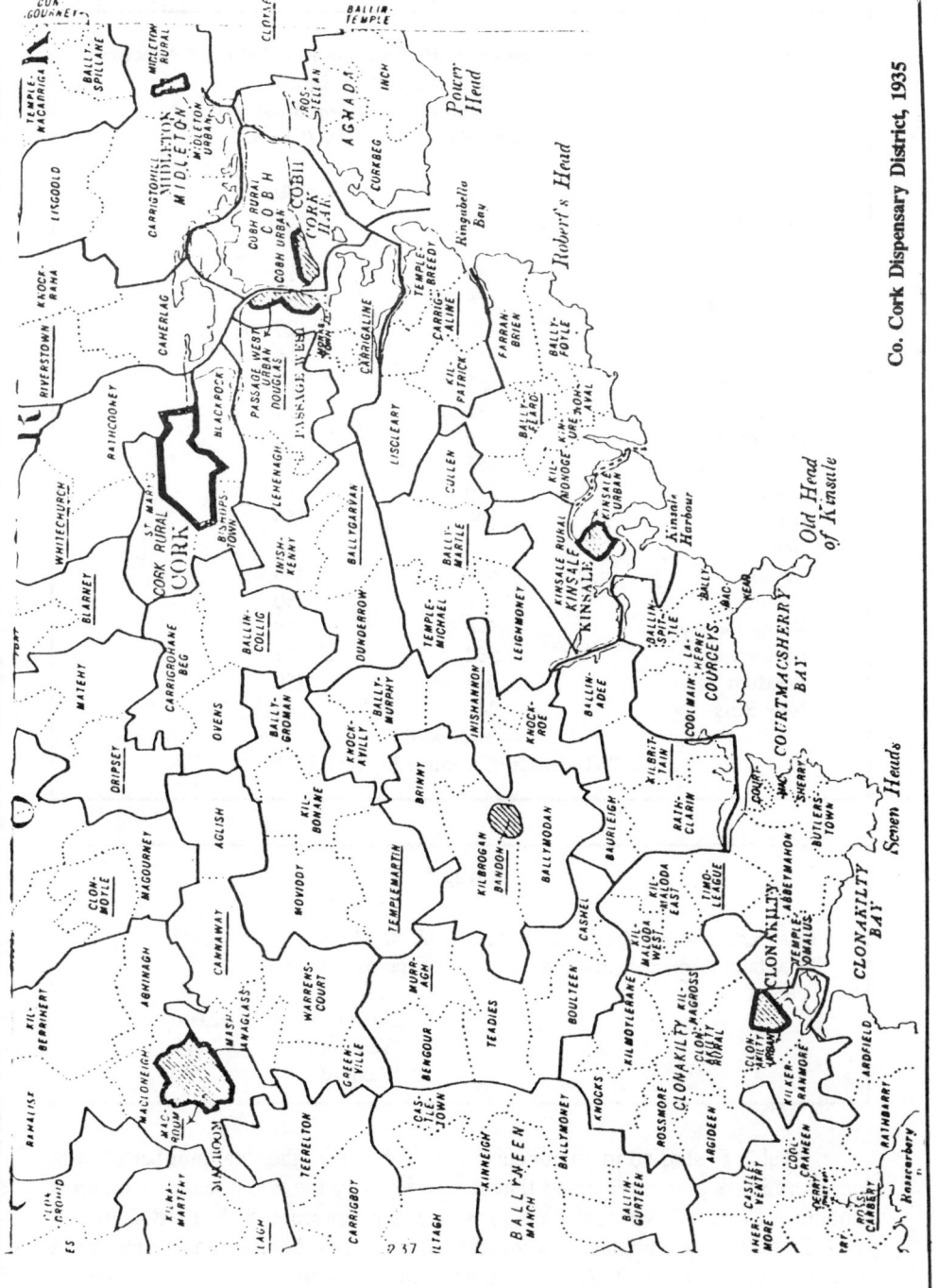

Table 6. No. Of Farm Labourers In Co. Cork ITGWU Branches Contrasted With Selected Other Branches

Branch	Total Branch Membership	Farm labourers In Branch	
Bishopstown	80	80	
Blarney Mens (Woollen Mls)	194	4	
Bantry	184	20	*
Buttevant	50	14	
Ballincollig	116	80	
Charleville	290	120	
Cobh	151	16	
Millstreet	35	33	
Riverstown	83	19	
Skibbereen	136	16	
Whitechurch	155	122	
Youghal	240	50	*
Bandon	300	150	*
Baldoyle	583	528	
Lucan	688	450	
Swords	350	250	
Kilmacthomas	544	458	
Dungarvan	582	231	
Wexford Town	1018	250	
New Ross	340	45	

* — Estimated
ITGWU census of membership 30.6.1918.

Table 7.

Total farm labourer membership of ITGWU, 30.7.19:	9,634	
Total farm labourer membership per county approximately:		
Cork	700	
Dublin	2,000	
Waterford	800	+
Wexford	300	+

Table 6, studied in conjunction with Table 7 on the total number of farm labourers in each county, shows that proportionately the two counties with most labourers, Cork and Wexford, were grossly under-represented. In 1918, Cork had over 20,000 farm labourers compared to Dublin's 5,000+ and Waterford's 4,500+, yet there were 2,000 labourers in the union in Dublin, 800+ in

Waterford, but only 700 in Cork. Similarly, Wexford had over 8,000 farm labourers but only 300+ in the Transport Union. The discrepancy is explained by the appeal of the older associations in Cork and Wexford (Figures for total labourer numbers, estimates from 1911 **Census of Population**, Occupations Volume, Table 20; ibid., p.14-15). That argument is reinforced when one considers that the Cork *city* membership of 4,042 was proportionately satisfactory in terms of a total union membership of 43,788 on the same date.

Not all opposition to the Transport Union ended in Co. Cork in September 1918. Patrick Bradley and his Cork City and County LLA continued in competition with increasing bitterness. When Florence O'Sullivan's letter recommending to the South Kilmurry branch to join the ITGWU appeared in the **Examiner**, Bradley responded immediately with a letter requesting the editor to make clear that neither Mr. O'Sullivan nor South Kilmurry had any connection with his association (CE, 14.9.18). Bradley's main efforts during 1918 were directed towards the recuperation of arrears, and he kept the labourers informed of the achievements of his association with constant advertisements in the local newspapers. He capitalised on his co-option to the Town Council in January, 1918 as well as his other public positions in exuberant notices such as "Wages! Wages! Wages! Over £300 recovered by the Land and Labour Association, 97 Patrick Street, Cork. President P.J. Bradley, TC, member AWB." (CE, 4.5.18; 15.4.18; 8.6.18.)

Even though the ITGWU expanded continuously in the second half of 1918, bringing its number of branches in *County* Cork to 25 (see ITGWU indexed list of branches 1909-22, MS 7282, NLI,) by the end of that year, Bradley still claimed in January 1919 that he now had "the largest and most effective rural workers' union in the south of Ireland" (CE, 7.1.19) He went on to criticize the Transport Union in the same speech, but then attempted to compete with them in rhetoric:

"They would soon have a combination of labour in Ireland, and if justice were not done to the working classes, democracy would next speak with the Red Flag floating over their heads, and then they would have the capitalists and employers do their duty" (ibid.).

The difference between the two organisations was that the Transport Union was willing to back its claim with strike action. The first strike came at Fermoy 12.3.19 when farmers failed to respond to detailed demands for the yearly contract (see Chapter 3). Bradley would not condone such action and attacked the ITGWU bitterly: "some workers were led by men who knew nothing about agricultural matters, and who plunged them into strikes by making demands which were unreasonable and impracticable at the moment. Such leaders did an injustice to the workers and the community, and created ill feeling between the farmers and the workers instead of cultivating the best spirit possible between them... the men he had in mind were not agricultural labourers and were never engaged in agricultural pursuits. Some of them were political organisers, paid organisers, and what object they could have in misleading any body of men would be for the workers in time to settle for themselves... all the labourers' representatives [on the AWB] had done their best with the exception of Mr. Foran who did not attend the meetings regularly..." (CE, 16.8.19).

Bradley defended the AWB against the attacks of the ITGWU, claiming it had recovered £23,076 for labourers up to 25.7.19 (CE, 30.7.19). Such defence of the Board did him no harm in the eyes of the Department of Agriculture, because when the names of the members of the newly established District Wages Committee for Co. Cork were announced, three of the four were Bradley's nominees.

However, as the Transport Union's strike movement became more and more successful on the farms, less was heard of the Cork City and County LLA. Bradley, running as an independent in the Cork central electoral district, lost his Town Council seat in the elections of January, 1920. Tadg Barry of the Transport Union, on the other hand — the "paid organiser" of farm labourers — was elected in the neighbouring Blarney Street/Sunday's Well area on the joint ITGWU/Sinn Fein ticket (CE, 19.1.20). By mid-1920, those Land and Labour branches that still survived were obliged to recognise the co-existence of the Transport Union. Thus the Mogeely branch LLA, with over 100 members in attendance, decided on 6 July, 1920 to work at threshing machines only with members of the LLA *or* Transport Union (CE, 7.7.20).

LABOUR IN NORTH KERRY

On Tuesday morning last the "Wage crisis in Newtownsandes, Co Kerry. At course in Newtownsandes, Co. Kerry. At 7.30 on that morning farmers to about 140 with pikes and other weapons were seen striding hurriedly towards the village, where they took up a position in the Main street. A short time after an equally large number of labourers, armed with sticks, also arrived in the village. For some considerable time excitement ran high, and on more than one occasion it was feared that the contending element would get into conflict. The Rev Father M. Keane, P.P., after much persuasion, succeeded in getting the parties to meet by delegation, as a result of which a satisfactory settlement was arrived at.

From Cork Examiner, 2.5.1919

chapter three

The Zenith Of Trade Unionism On The Farm, 1919-20

A census of membership taken by the ITGWU on 31 January, 1920 claimed 30,292 farm labourers fully paid up, with another 20,000 who were temporarily out of work for winter months (ITGWU census of membership in **Annual Report** 1920 and **Watchword of Labour**, 25.9.1920) This compared with a total of 9,643 farm workers on 30 June, 1918. During 1919 and 1920, the ITGWU led those farm workers on a vigorous campaign that included strikes for wage increases and improved working conditions. The emblems, anthems and rhetoric of revolutionary socialism were fully employed.

The analysis of the events of those years that follows goes into exhaustive detail on the campaign for a few shillings here and the struggle to work one hour per day less there. But to see the significance of the events simply in such terms would be to miss the point. While not as significant as Trotsky in his armoured train in Russia during these years, the union organiser on his bicycle in Cork and other counties was also attempting to make a revolution. He was out to raise the standard of living of the rural worker. The achievement of that would have been a revolution because it would have transformed the social status of the agricultural labourer.

Before the War, this labourer had been a member of a relatively small, despised class with low social status. Improved wages, proper working conditions and a signed contract would have changed his own and other people's pereception of his position in the rural community. Such would have accomplished a revolution.

During 1917 and 1918 the ITGWU was mainly concerned with establishing new rural branches and bringing LLA members into the Union. The objective in those years was to compel the farmer to pay the AWB minimum rate. Since there was legal backing for that rate of pay, most farmers were not inclined to risk a strike on the issue. There were some strikes in 1918, however, in Cork as in other counties. At harvest time a strike took place at Dungarvan to recover arrears under AWB rates, and following arbitration £78 back money was awarded (Greaves, p.193). The farmers of Callan, Co. Kilkenny refused to negotiate on the arrears issue, and in the ensuing strike the harvest came near to being lost. In Co. Laois the Transport Union ran a campaign against the provision of drink at harvesting, claiming that the farmers who supplied it made an excessive profit. In Co. Cork farm labourers also experienced the first stirrings of strike action in 1918 (ibid.). A dispute at Charleville, which started with a demand for wage increases from the bakers, soon encompassed all the Transport Union members in the area to the number of 290, including 120 farm labourers adjacent to the town. The strike dragged on for nine weeks before being submitted to arbitration on 26 August, 1918 (CE, 12.8.1918). Thus, farm workers and other interested parties throughout Co. Cork received proof that the ITGWU could sustain them over a long period out of work, and achieve results.

The trials and tribulations of the branch secretary in the newly formed branches catering mainly for farm labourers have been recorded in a letter from Patrick Buckley of the Cloghroe branch, six miles West of Cork City, to ITGWU head office in Dublin. Buckley himself was a labourer, and the letter was in response to another from HQ which expressed anxiety about the delay in receipt of branch contributions at head office. The branch was in existence for two months at this stage, and while membership number is not mentioned, it stood at 140 by the end of 1918.

"ITGWU
September 3rd 1918.   Cloghroe Branch

Dear Sir,
 I have told you before that it's fortnightly meetings we hold. It is on Sunday. I have to make collection and I have to do Mathey and Saint Annes one Sunday and Cloghroe and Inniscarra another Sunday. I has [sic] to get the Berrings done for me. As you know all this branch are Agricultural Labourers and there are some of them I won't see for 4 or 5 weeks now, as they are gone to different places harvesting. I was at Cloghroe on the 25 [sic] and such rain never fell and only 6 members turned up. Last Sunday [sic] meeting I had to postpone owing to a Gaelic League concert by orders from Cork Branch as you will see by enclosed telegram. You will have money for next Tuesday for the two weeks ending 27 [sic] . You aske [sic] me for the names of officers and committee. [Names and addresses of committee follow.]
P.S. We are to add 2 more to committee next meeting. We have some local trouble of our own at present.

                                                                                         P. Buckley
Excuse hurry as I am running for the post. I will write a long letter and explain all matters tomorrow night." (MS 13 948, William O'Brien Collection, NLI.)

From March, 1919 onwards the farm workers' wage movement achieved real momentum. The policy adopted by the Executive Committee of the Transport Union was to press demands in as many districts as possible. The demands were strongly opposed so that the strikes of 1919 were marked by great bitterness and violent incidents in many counties, Cork being no exception. The tactics of Ribbonism (see J.J. Lee, **The Ribbonmen** in T.D. Williams (ed) **Secret Societies in Ireland**) accompanied an open trade union agitation. Since many of the incidents have not received notice from historians, it is necessary to describe them at some length. To those who would suggest that this is merely selecting and highlighting sensational incidents, it should be stressed that such occurrences were but the strongest manifestations of widespread hostility.

Bad feeling was created in North Kerry in March, 1919 with the rejection of the demand by Lixnaw labourers for 25/- per week plus diet. The strike which followed seriously hampered spring work, while six creameries were closed down when the workers there went out in sympathy. Though the strike was settled on 9 April, the level of feeling aroused in the area was seen three weeks later when matters came to a head in another North Kerry district. At 7.30 on the morning of 29 April, 1919 about 140 farmers with pikes and what the **Examiner** called other "weapons" were seen "striding hurriedly towards the village of Newtownsandes where they took up a position in the main street. A short time after an equally large number of labourers armed with sticks, also arrived in the village. For some considerable time excitement ran high, and on more than one occasion it was feared that the contending elements would get into conflict" After much persuasion, Fr. M. Keane PP, succeeded in getting the parties to meet by delegation, as a result of which a settlement was arrived at (CE, 2.5.1919).

At the beginning of April, labourers in East Donegal, members of the National Amalgamated Union of Labour, struck for wage increases. Farmers responded with a lock-out, and work was carried out in places under the protection of guns carried by farmers, while there were allegations that farmers fired at pickets. Non-strikers were assaulted by pickets (CE, 12.4.19).

A strike at Celbridge, Co. Kildare towards the end of June 1919, involving 60 labourers, took a serious turn on 6 July when Kildare Farmers Union decided to lock out all Transport Union members in the county (CE, 7.7.19; 26.7.19; 6.8.19). By 26 July, 2,700 labourers were out in Kildare and Meath, while Dublin port was affected on 5 August. The ferocity of the struggle can be gauged from the fact that on 15 August the 3.30 am goods train was derailed at a bend on a steep incline, 30 wagons being completely smashed. The target in fact had been a cattle special booked for a northern port from Navan a few hours later (CE, 18.8, 22.8, 25.8.1919). Breaking the rail at that particular location took the work of 10 men and would certainly have led to the slaughter of a huge number of cattle had the intended train been derailed.

The ITGWU's record of events in the **Annual Report 1919** is interesting because it does not mention the destruction of the train: "The fight was carried through by the labourers with a vigour and discipline that commanded success... The turning point in the struggle was the success of the Union in Belfast in blocking the sale of a special trainload of cattle from Meath, which had to be returned to the pastures. Good settlements were finally effected in each county and the basis of future improvements securely laid in the enhanced prestige of the Union and the establishment of its claim to be the premier Irish Union for agricultural workers." (p.7-8.)

In mid-November a dispute which was in progress in Kilmallock on the question of a harvest bonus developed into a conflict in which blows were freely exchanged between farmers and labourers. (CE, 13.11.19). In November also, corn and hay to the value of between £2-£3,000 was totally destroyed in a malicious fire at Crotta, Lixnaw, Co. Kerry. The land had been put up for sale the previous summer, but the sale had fallen through, owing to a demonstration of the landless people of the district who were agitating for the parcelling out of the lands amongst them. (CE, 26.11.19). Whether or not the labourers were responsible for the fire, the two events were connected by local people, thus creating bitterness and hostility.

The somewhat better known "Battle of Fenor" in Co. Waterford also occurred in November 1919 (see Emmet O'Connor, *Saothar vi*, p.41). A dispute over harvest bonus led to a general lockout of labourers on 22 November. When the farmers attempted to proceed with threshing themselves, conflict erupted. When a threshing machine was being escorted by 100 constables and 21 "other" policemen to the farm of Joseph Widgers, they were confronted by 250-300 men with a red flag and led by Nicholas Phelan, Waterford Co. Secretary, ITGWU. A fierce riot ensued, following which the labourers, as they retreated, destroyed 80 tons of first and second crop hay, over 400 barrels of oats and barley, and gutted a large barn, all the property of Mr. Widger, and for which £3,285 compensation was paid later from the rates (CE, 26.11, 29.11.19; 15.12.19; 19.2.1920).

Such outrages also occurred in Co. Cork. The **Annual Report** of Cork Farmers' Union (CFU) for 1919 suggests the seriousness of the situation:

FARM LABOUR STRIKE.
LINE TORN UP.
TRAIN DERAILED.

Sensational developments occurred in connection with the Meath farm labourers' strike on Friday night. On the Meath branch line of the G.N.R. between Beauparc and Navan, the rails were lifted up at a bend on a steep incline, with the result that the 3.50 a.m. goods train to Drogheda was derailed and smashed. Thirty waggons were strewn about the line in all sorts of positions, some of them completely smashed, and all of them badly damaged. The engine-driver, fireman and guard were fortunate to escape with a severe shaking.

The guard had his brakes on hard at the time, and to this fact he attributes the escape of his van and his own luck. The affair caused considerable excitement in Drogheda on Saturday, and was the principal topic of conversation in the market. The branch line traffic was completely held up on Saturday. The 10 o'clock passenger train did not leave Drogheda, and the train from Oldcastle was unable to get beyond Navan.

The mails for the Co. Meath arriving at Drogheda were sent off by motor. At 11 o'clock on Saturday an accident train from Dundalk, with a breakdown gang, passed through to the scene of the outrage. Armed troops were also hurriedly dispatched there. It is stated that a cattle special booked from Navan to a Northern port was to have left Navan early on Saturday morning, and it was this train that it was intended to destroy.

The Naval correspondent of the "Sunday Independent" wires:—The Great Northern Railway line between Beauparc and Navan was torn up on Friday morning, and a goods train totally wrecked. All railway traffic is suspended. An accident train and a breakdown gang from the Broadstone is on the way, also one from Dundalk. The line is expected to be cleared by Tuesday

From Cork Examiner, 18.8.1919

"In some districts farmers have had to get rid of their dairy stock owing to labour troubles... Where farm produce had been wantonly burned the destruction might have been largely prevented had active vigilance committees been appointed in disturbed areas. (CE, 23.2.1920.)

The outrage connected with one dispute in Cork is well documented. At the beginning of July, the ITGWU farm labourers in Churchtown demanded an 8/- per week increase for a four-month period. When this was refused a general strike of 150 labourers in Churchtown and neighbouring Buttevant followed on 7 July 1919. They were joined in sympathy strike by the creamery workers. Two days later a large contingent marched from Buttevant to Churchtown carrying a red banner inscribed, "Workers of the world unite. The unorganised worker is the slave of his employer".

Local farmers and their sons meanwhile carted the milk to the creamery every day and, with the assistance of the local creamery manager, separated the milk and made butter and cheese. Then on 11 July, a farmer's son, who brought another farmer's milk to the creamery with his own, was fired on about 100 yards from Churchtown police barracks. The shots narrowly missed him but killed the jennet he was leading. The general consternation which followed was increased by the fact that many farmers had several fields of hay lying on the sward, with over 50 pairs of horses idle, while it was reported that the majority of the workers in the district were men with large families, who would suffer great distress from a continuance of the dispute.

By 17 July, the majority of servant girls in Buttevant parish had come out in sympathy with the men. The ITGWU county organiser, Tadg Barry, stiffened the challenge to farmers at that stage when he wrote to the **Examiner**:

"Perhaps the impecuniosity of the labourer is being depended on to win for our opponents, but the Transport Union has now given its full sanction to the fight, and means to show that the agitation which our predecessors carried on for the 'land for the people' means not the 'land for the farmers' as some of them think, but that its fruits shall be the co-operative property of those whose labour produce those fruits..." (CE, 21.7.19).

Settlement was agreed to 16 July in Churchtown and in Buttevant four days later, the main terms in each case being a 4s. increase along with a £3 bonus in November (CE, 12, 16, 17, 18, 21.7.19).

While such dramatic scenes were not enacted, there is evidence of the bitterness that marked other disputes in Co. Cork during 1919 also. The Inniscarra Farmers Association resented the demand to negotiate where they had previously dictated terms and refused to recognise the Transport Union. The local ITGWU branch had put forward their claim based on the "county demand" for that year on 5 March (CE, 5.3.1919). The county demand was:

"30/- a week, a house free, half an acre of garden, seeded, tilled and manured, a quart of new milk a day, and 30 cwt of coal a year, six days work of 9 hours per day. One shilling per hour overtime. No settlement to be made without communicating with union secretary. Not to work with non-Union men. To work for no other farmer except employer, except when casual labour is unobtainable. To follow only employer's reaper and binder. When taking place of casual labourers in the case already stated, to work for 5s. a day and nothing less. No distinction at table. Not to take up a position which another member is negotiating for. A living wage for Women and Girls. " (CE, 12.5.1919).

Inniscarra Farmers Union ignored these demands and a strike followed at the end of April. Local Sinn Fein members felt the Farmers Union behaved so arrogantly that the mid-Cork Irish Volunteers were moved to "indignantly resent the insult offered to our worthy representative, Mr. Terence Mac Swiney TDE, by members of the Inniscarra Farmers Union" in refusing to accept him as an arbitrator (CE, 12.5.19). Mac Swiney was greatly alarmed at the split in nationalist ranks in the parish and was obliged to devote much time and energy to prevent a deterioration. He could understand, he said, strikes taking place now and again in the city, but it was from the country that they got their food, and if they had strikes in the country the land would go out of tillage. "No man had a right to advocate force on the part of one body of Irishmen against another (applause)". He understood that his actions had been misrepresented, but he had now given his views on the matter so that they could understand how to act in the future (ibid.).

Even where newspaper reports attempted to play down the existence of antagonism, it is possible to detect it. Thus, with regard to a Lehenagh farm dispute, on the outskirts of Cork city, in August, it was reported that after a three-hour discussion the question of an advance in wages was satisfactorily settled. "A very pleasing feature of the proceedings was the entire absence of anything in the shape of recriminations", we are told, but then we gather that one farmer proved recalcitrant, whose workers were then on strike and he himself under police protection (CE, 2.8.19). Similarly, when the Whitechurch dispute was settled at the beginning of July, Tadg Barry, in thanking Fr. Sheehan, the arbitrator, said the priest's action had "saved bloodshed". He hoped the workers would "continue as they were, and keep cool and not give way to any incitement" (CE, 2.7.19).

Table 8 shows the level of strike activity in Co. Cork during 1919. The amount of activity is comparable with the other advanced counties, Dublin, Kildare and Meath, but the significant variation is that while settlements on a county basis were achieved in Dublin in May and in Kildare and Meath in August, the Cork agreements were still very much on a district basis. Table 9 emphasises even further how the differing conditions existing in the county were reflected in the varying demands of union branches. Bad feeling was engendered by a strike threat in farming, even if the strike was later avoided.

Table 8. Farm Strikes In County Cork, 1919

ITGWU Branch	Date Of Strike	Duration	Demands	Settlement Terms
Fermoy	12.3.1919	5 days	County Demand (see p.47-8)	22/- Plus Perquisites 15/- for servant boys 2/6 for Sunday
Inniscarra	Before 27.4.1919	2 weeks+	County Demand	
Whitechurch		Until 1.7.19	One farmer broke previous agreement re claim of a farmer on a bound man at end of year's service	Mediator judged farmer had no claim on a man who worked for him previous year and finished his service
Churchtown & Buttevant	7.7.1919	Until 16.7 & 20.7	35/- without diet to bound men; 27/- with diet, £4 bonus for boarded men	Increase of 4/- a week and equivalent plus £3 harvest bonus
Lehenagh	18.8.1919	1 week	4/- increase for those 4 men who were refused it	4/- increase granted
Kinsale Junction	Before 27/8	At least 4 days	250 demanded 5/- increase 2/6 per day for transferred men no non-union men	Offered 31/- per week cash
Ballindee		Until 27.8.19	£5 harvest bonus	£4 bonus and 2/6 for borrowed men
Tullyland Bandon	25.8.1919	2 days	£5 harvest bonus	£4 bonus

Cork Examiner 12.3.19; 2,12.5.19; 2, 8, 12, 14.7.19; 25, 28, 29.8.19; **Voice of Labour** 1919, passim.

Table 9. Threatened farm strikes in Co. Cork, 1919

ITGWU	Date Of Notice	Demands
Whitechurch	13.3.1919	County Demand (See page 47-8)
Kildorrery	13.3.1919	County Demand
Newmarket	8.4.1919	35/- without board, 18/- including full board, no non-union men to work with union men
Castlemagner	19.7.1919	Casual labourers 10/- per day without board, 10/- for going to fair, 1/- overtime, 9 hour day
Ballyclough	19.7.1919	5/- cored men per day, 5/- for going to a fair, 1/- overtime per hour, no non-union men
Kanturk	27.7.1919	£5 harvest bonus, 5/- a day for borrowed men, no non-union men to work with union men
Rathcormac	13.8.1919	During harvesting 10/- a day with meals for casuals, 13/- without meals, yearly men 5/- extra
Cloghroe	13.8.1919	5/- increase granted
Ballincollig & Bishopstown	13.8.1919	5/- increase granted
Riverstown	23.8.1919	Granted £3 harvest bonus, borrowed men 3/- a day
Doneraile	27.8.1919	No union men to work with non-union men
Great Island (Cobh)	27.8.1919	£2 per week plus harvest bonus
Liscarroll	29.8.1919	5/- per day for borrowed men; no non-union men with union men, overtime after 6 o'clock
Ballincollig	29.8.1919	Some farmers failing to honour agreement of 13/8 (see above)
Watergrass Hill	4.9.1919	Agreed £3 harvest bonus, 3/- per day for borrowed men, overtime after 6 pm
Freemont	5.9.1919	5/- for borrowed men
Castlemagner	5.9.1919	As for 19.7.19 above
South Kilmurry	11.9.1919	£5 bonus without board, £3 with board
Aghada	13.9.1919	5/- increase all round, 5/- per day for borrowed men
Churchtown	13.9.1919	No union men to work with non-union men

Cork Examiner as per dates listed in column 2; **Voice of Labour** 1919 passim

The farm wage struggle of 1920 was marked throughout Ireland by several new developments. Firstly, the IFU was becoming increasingly vigorous and well-organised. Thus CFU reported that, at the end of January 1919, it consisted of 12 branches with a total membership of 500. By mid-February 1920, however, this had grown to 51 branches with a membership of betweeen 3,000 and 4,000, with the expectation of doubling that number by the end of 1920 (CFU **Annual Report**, 1919, CE, 23.2.20). It was no coincidence that all these branches were in the parishes where the ITGWU existed. The mood of some farmers throughout the country in 1920 was indicated by the manifesto of Wexford Farmers' Association, issued in May, for the establishment of a Farmers' Freedom Force (FFF) "as a national bulwark against Labour, Socialism and Bolshevism". This certainly gave a new meaning to the '3Fs'. William O'Brien of the ITGWU responded to the proposal with the challenge: "There are 50,000 farm labourers in the ITGWU and if the farmers are looking for a fight we'll give it to them" (ibid.). Cork Farmers' Union, though some misgivings were expressed, unanimously "urges the F.U. branches to assist in forming FFF's for the purpose of self defence" (CE, 3.7.20).

On the other hand, the growth of Farmers' Unions facilitated county wage agreements. Thus a county agreement was signed in Dublin after a two-week strike in March, giving 43/- outdoor for a 54 hour week, with £3 harvest bonus and a weekly half-holiday (CE, 1.4.20). Similarly, a county agreement in Waterford in May 1920 gave 38/6 outdoor for a seven-day week, with proportionate rates for those under 20 and for indoor workers. The size of Co. Cork, and the diversity of conditions within it, made a county settlement all the more difficult, but steps were taken in that direction in 1920.

Another notable feature during the first half of 1920 was that, despite the sabre-rattling of the proposed FFF, moves towards conciliation were taking place because of the tense political situation. Following a series of strikes in May, 1920, Limerick farmers decided to invite the ITGWU to appoint six representatives to a committee with a like number of Farmers' Union members. At the beginning of March, eighteen Cork ITGWU branches demanded a 10/- increase from 25 March. This was ignored but, after a short strike in the Liberties, a conciliation committee was established which granted a top rate of 42/6 for 54 hours outdoor, and 24/- indoor (CE, 6.4.20).

But at the same time, the increasing determination of farmers to withstand demands was evident in the fact that Ballincollig, which was a neighbouring parish to Bishopstown (part of Liberties), and had continuously moved in line with it during 1919, did not achieve an increase until Bishopstown was granted the Liberties terms. Even when Ballincollig achieved its increase the rate was less than in the Liberties, being at maximum 41/1 outdoor and 22/- indoor (CE, 6.4.20).

It took longer to bring about negotiations in North-east Cork in April, where the strikes were vigorously fought by both sides. Tadg Barry was present in the region for the duration of the strike, indicating the determination of the Transport Union. The strike started in Kilavullen on 12 May for 36/- a week indoor, and dragged on for two weeks. Doneraile followed on the 13th, and from there it spread to Castletownroche, where a "prolonged battle" seemed inevitable, until the arrival home from Mountjoy of Thomas Hunter, the Sinn Fein TD, prompted peace talks (CE, 4.5.20).

The growing incidence of terrorism and consequent lawlessness in Co. Cork from June 1920 onwards greatly influenced labour agitation. By mid-April 1920, 223 RIC barracks had been destroyed by the IRA, nine in Co. Cork on the single weekend of 5.4.20 (CE, 10.5.20). This led to increasingly ferocious retaliations by the Black and Tans. Against such a background, Sinn Fein arbitration courts stepped in immediately strike notice was issued in the South, in an effort to keep a united nationalist front at all costs.

Thus, when a farm strike was three days in progress in Fermoy, both sides agreed to Sinn Fein Arbitration on 3 May (CE, 6.7.20). Similarly, when a strike occurred in the Liberties district at the start of September, the men had to return to work after four days at the request of a Sinn Fein arbitration court. The chairman of the court reminded the labourers that "these were not peace times, and a strike in such matters would not be justified. They should avail of the machinery set up by the Republic for dealing with such matters and there was nothing to be gained by direct action" (CE, 8.9.20).

Two weeks later a Sinn Fein court arbitrated the dispute in the Ballygarvan district, producing a detailed recommendation in fifteen points (20.9.20). In eight other districts settlements were reached without strikes during September, 1920. These were Knockraha and Glounthaune, Ballyclogh, Liscarroll, Glanthane, South Kilmurry, Lyre, Coolclough and Aghinagh (CE, 7, 11, 21, 27, 29, 30.9.20; **Watchword of Labour** 18.9.20). In South Kilmurry, for example, the chairman of the Transport Union branch admitted that the £3 bonus agreed was not up to expectation but, having regard to the present unsettled condition of the country, strikes should be avoided if at all possible (ibid., 29.9.20).

Yet, despite all these peaceful settlements, August-September 1920 saw the greatest incidents of farm strikes ever in the county. The ITGWU **Annual Report** for 1920 considered these Cork strikes the most notable on Irish farms during the year, and calculated that almost 2,000 men were out in the different districts (p.8). The union felt that farmers had been taking advantage of the negotiating machinery in those districts to avoid a settlement.

Table 10. Cork Farm Strikes 1920

ITGWU Branch	Date Of	Duration	Demands	Settlement Terms
Liberties, including B'stown, Glasheen	Until 5.4.1920	A few days	10/- increase all round	6/- increase
Killavullen	12.4.1920	2 weeks	36/- per week + harvest bonus	33/- + £3 harvest bonus
Doneraile	13.4.1920	1 week	As above	As above, plus 37/- outdoor & proportionate equivalents
Castletownroche	Until 1.5.1920	1-2 weeks	As above	As above
Fermoy	Until 3.7.1920	3 days	Increase to 45/- outdoor	37/- outdoor, £4 harvest bonus
Churchtown	25.8.1920	1 week	Increase to 45/- & £5 harvest bonus	40/- outdoor max., £3 bonus
Buttevant	25.8.1920	4 days	As above	40/- outdoor, £4 harvest bonus
South Liberties B'town, Douglas, Lehenagh, R'town	Until 7.9.1920	4 days +	15/- over AWB rate & £5 harvest bonus	46/- outdoor, 6 days 26/- indoor
Fermoy	4.9.1920	1 week	That agreement (above) include indoor workers	5/- increase for indoor men
Kanturk	14.9.1920	A few days		7/6 per week increase £3 bonus
Aghabullogue	11.9.1920	10 days		Standard rate (30/-) + £5 rate bonus
Kilpatrick (Bandon)	10.9.1920	3 weeks+	40/- & £4 harvest bonus	Arbitration in October 1920 by Deputy Lord Mayor of Cork
Aghada	Mid Sept.	6 days		45/6 top rate, 26/- and 24/6 indoor men, no non-union labour to be employed

Cork Examiner, 6.4.1920, 4.5.1920, 28.8.1920, 3, 7, 15, 18, 21, 29.9.1920; Watchword of Labour, 18, 25.9.1920; 9.10.1920.

At least 7 separate strikes took place over August–September. Picketing was carried on vigorously by the workers, who controlled the entry of all vehicles to some areas. The slogans, emblems and rhetoric of the socialist revolution were much in evidence. That these strikes occurred at all was remarkable considering the political situation. On 2 August the Black and Tans had smashed up the ITGWU headquarters, the Connolly Memorial Hall at Camden Quay, Cork without any provocation. Clearly, to go on strike to the accompaniment of revolutionary emblems was inviting attention. It may not have been the Red Flag to the proverbial bull, but this dark and amber hound had already proven himself to be as ferocious as any bull.

A second factor which would have made the strikes unlikely was that, for each day of their duration in September, the people of Cork and many around the world were obsessed with the apparently imminent demise of Lord Mayor, Terence MacSwiney, who was on hunger strike in Brixton prison. To upset Cork and nationalist solidarity with a strike in such circumstances was brave indeed. Rural Cork ITGWU branches were as well represented as any other groups in the daily lengthening list of paid Masses for the Lord Mayor recorded in the **Cork Examiner**, but that did not deter them from pursuing their own interests also.

Churchtown labourers struck on 25 August, from where the strike spread to Buttevant. The Transport Union workers then closed the local creamery and hoisted the Red Flag from the highest vantage point. They declared that if a settlement were not speedily effected, they would take over the running of the creamery themselves. Over 400 men were involved, and large numbers of them were concentrated in various parts of Churchtown village, while picketing was being conducted throughout the entire parish. A number of farmers who took their milk to Liscarroll creamery had to return with the same when the Transport Union stopped delivery at the creamery. Three calf buyers who came to the district were ordered to leave, which they did without transacting any business. After a week's strike, the Churchtown labourers decided that all the servant girls in the parish would be called out and that, according to the **Examiner** correspondent, "will bring matters to a climax". The strike was settled by granting 40/- top rate in both areas, with a £4 harvest bonus in Buttevant and £3 in Churchtown (CE, 28, 31.8.1918).

The organisation of the labourers was equally impressive in other districts. The ITGWU weekly newspaper was euphoric about the performance of the workers in Aghada. "They showed a discipline, determination and organised efficiency highly commendable. For six days the Red Guards held complete sway over this large tract of countryside, while only those commodities for which permits had been received could enter or leave the affected area." (**Watchword of Labour**, 25.9.20.)

As a result of the strikes, labourers in Rochestown and Doughcloyne received 57/6 top rate, in the North Liberties 52/6 and 46/- in several other districts. This meant that by the end of September 1920, farm labourers in those areas of Co. Cork adjacent to the City were the best paid farm workers in Ireland.

Confidence was at an all-time high among the rural workers who felt they could impose their demands on farmers despite the pleas from the IRA for nationalist unity. The tactics used were a combination of agrarian crime and militant trade unionism. Thus, when the **Watchword of Labour** wrote of the "determination" of the Aghada labourers, what actually occurred was that farmers had been intimidated by fear of the consequences of not granting the demands. The 'Red Guards' were those on picket duty along the roads who refused to allow vehicles to pass. In the absence of police protection, drivers were unwilling to risk passing the pickets.

The question arises as to whether the enthusiasm for the Red Flag was social revolutionary fervour or militant trade unionism. There was a growing working class culture in 1920 which openly identified with the Red Flag and which took inspiration from the Russian Revolution. The emphasis, however, was on the immediate demands for better wages and improved working conditions. Though the Red Flag flew over Churchtown, it was removed when the wage increase and harvest bonus were granted. It was nonetheless a "mighty agiation", which "struck fear into the heart of Republicans" (Fitzpatrick, **The Disappearance of the Irish Agricultural Labourer, 1841-1912,** *Irish Economic and Social History*, vii, 1980). It ignored the proclamation which the Dail had issued on 29th June—

"That the present time when the Irish people are locked in a life and death struggle with their traditional enemy, is ill chosen for the stirring up of strife amongst our fellow countrymen..." (cited in M.A.G. O'Tuathaigh **The Land Question, Politics and Irish Society, 1922-1960,** in P.J. Drudy (ed.) **Irish Studies 2, Ireland: Land Politics & People**, p.171).

The response from the Cork correspondent of the **Watchword of Labour** was dismissive. "...The spectacle of unanimity shown by the Farmers' Union — Sinn Fein and the Unionists — had a most edifying effect on the proletariat of Aghada, and the Red Guards appreciated with acclamation when it was pointed out how the facetious political feuds of these people were sunk... — to compel the labourer to exist on the 32/6 minimum wage..." (25.9.1920).

The 1920 wage campaign was to be the zenith of trade unionism on Cork farms. From November onwards to July 1921 the ever worsening warfare and terrorism, with the curfews, arrests, and destruction of meeting places, made union activity extremely hazardous and difficult. In addition, the advent of agricultural recession was accompanied by growing unemployment, which changed the parameters of relationships on the farm back to the pre-War position. It is now necessary to examine how the combination of war and economic depression led to the defeat of trade unionism on the farm.

chapter four

The Defeat Of Trade Unionism On The Farm 1921-23

The history of rural trade unionism from 1921 to '23 falls into four distinct phases. The final months of the War of Independence, November 1920–July 1921, greatly disrupted all economic and social life in Munster counties. The earlier open identification of the ITGWU with the Volunteers meant that the union's activities would be the object of close attention from the Black and Tans. Rural union branches were consequently badly affected during those first six months of 1921. The eleven months from the Truce to the start of the Civil War, however, witnessed a strong revival in activity and widespread farm strikes. Both labourers and farmers attempted to use their connections with the Republican police and IRA during this time to gain advantage over the opponent in a dispute.

The third distinct phase was the Civil War. This wreaked havoc with union organisation in Munster counties once more, and left a legacy of apathy and disillusionment. Finally, as the struggles between farm workers and employers became even more bitter during the spring and summer of 1923, strikers found themselves confronted with the Free State Army and police.

Throughout 1921-23 rising unemployment was a constant factor which compounded the effects of warfare, forcing the Transport Union out of the countryside at the end of 1923.

Following the wave of farm strikes of September 1920, the ITGWU newspaper, **Watchword of Labour**, declared that the wage campaign in Cork had been brought to a satisfactory conclusion for that year (9.10.1920). No further trouble would therefore be anticipated until the spring of 1921. In any case, winter farm strikes were undesirable from the workers' viewpoint because, when the harvest was saved and threshing over, farming operations wound down from November to February. An employer would be in a better bargaining position during those months and could allow a dispute to drag on.

By the spring of 1921, however, circumstances had changed completely. The third and bloodiest phase of the War of Independence dominated as terror and ambush was matched by counter-terror and "official reprisals". By January 1921, the ITGWU had already recorded that, through the country, three branch secretaries had been shot, thirty-two were in jail, while eight branch premises had been destroyed (Greaves, p.294). In some rural areas branch meetings were now held in remote cowsheds at night. By July 1921, out of 583 Transport Union branches on the roll, 115 had totally collapsed.

Nowhere had the fighting and destruction been more intense than in Co. Cork. Terence MacSwiney's death on 25 October greatly heightened emotions. On the night of 12 November, the Black and Tans singled out the Cork Transport Union headquarters on Camden Quay, and virtually destroyed the entire building by fire.

The killing of two lorry loads of Auxiliaries on 28 November at Kilmichael by Tom Barry's Flying Column meant that the population had to steel itself for reprisal. On 10 December, martial law was proclaimed in Cork and neighbouring counties. The next night saw the burning and destruction of a large part of the city centre. On 30 January 1921, Tadg Barry was arrested at a meeting of the city council, taken to Spike Island and subsequently transferred to Balykinlar internment camp. He was shot dead there at the end of 1921 by a sentry (possibly accidentally). His absence during 1921 was a severe blow to the Transport Union in the city and county.

This background has been sketched to illustrate the difficulties of the period and to demonstrate that the continued vigorous pressing of their demands by Cork farm workers and farmers in such circumstances was remarkable. Analysis of newspaper reports and notices between January and July 1921 shows that at least 32 Cork rural branches of the Transport Union were active in pressing demands for farm workers. Furthermore, progress was actually made in certain aspects of organisation. For example, on 23 March 1921, seven branches — Aghabullogue, Aghinagh, Cloghroe, Cloughduv, Dripsey, Donoughmore and Ovens — put forward a uniform demand for £2 per week wages and a list of other requirements (CE, 23.3.21). That was overcoming what had been noted as a major problem in the country during the previous years, when the diversity of demands from parish to parish made joint action difficult. For those seven branches covering such a wide area in mid-Cork (see Map on Pages 38-39) to be able to formulate a uniform demand was itself an advance.

The Dail government utterly deplored any strike in this "hour of national crisis" and prevailed in forcing arbitration in those instances where a farm strike was notified. Thus, the settlement of a dispute in the North Liberties of Cork (St. Mary's, Hollyhill, Dublin Hill, Glanmire) in mid-April 1921 set an important example. The arbitration court declared that:

> "...all sections of the community must be prepared for sacrifice, internecine strife, especially such as affects vital food supplies of the Irish people, is to be strongly deprecated... We therefore strongly urge the formation of District Joint Committees consisting of say three representatives of the farmers and three of the workers, perhaps with the help of the clergy, whose function it would be to adjust minor differences... and in friendly personal intercourse to cultivate a spirit of mutual respect and Christian charity..." (CE, 19.4.21).

A detailed award of eleven points was then published by the court. The top wage in the North Liberties was settled at 47/6 (ibid.), which was a *reduction* of 5/- from what had been achieved in the district by the strike of the previous September. The justification for the reduction was that the prices of agricultural produce had peaked in 1920 and the index figure for the cost of living had also turned downwards. Table 11 indicates the decline in agricultural wholesale prices.

Table 11. Index Of Irish Agricultural Wholesale Prices

Year	Wheat	Oats	Barley	Potatoes	Butter	Eggs	Beef	Mutton
1919	150	334	357	466	298	1,013	292	333
1920	189	347	331	630	338	934	330	412
1921	136	231	196	382	218	675	258	299

Adapted from Thomas Barrington, **A review of Irish agricultural prices,** JSSISI 1925-6, p.253

Once an example in wage reduction had been set, employers in neighbouring parishes attempted to follow. Thus, two weeks after the North Liberties settlement, labourers in the Lehenagh district of the South Liberties issued strike notice when wages were reduced by 4/6 without negotiation. The dispute was settled without a strike, however. The issue in most districts then became one of workers resisting employers' demands for reductions, rather than seeking further increases.

With agricultural recession came unemployment, so that the early months of 1921 also saw Cork rural union branches attempting to regulate the influx of labourers from other areas. At least fourteen Cork branches had notices in the **Examiner,** between January and July 1921, warning outsiders to "communicate with the branch secretary before taking up labouring jobs in the parish" (CE, 5.1.21, 15.1.21, 29.1.21, 23.2.21, 4.3.21, 7.3.21, 9.3.21, 12.3.21, 17.3.21, 18, 19, 23.3.21, 26.4.21, 9.7.21).

Another suggested antidote to unemployment was to demand more tillage because it was labour intensive. At least seven Cork branches put notices in the **Examiner** during the first six months of 1921 urging farmers to give 30% of their land to tillage "as the principals of the country at the present time are men, not bullocks" (CE, 21.1.21, 11, 23.2.21, 3.3.21, 7.3.21, 7.4.21).

There was a severe blow to this latter demand and a detrimental blow to the farm labourers' security when it was revealed without notice on 7 June 1921 that the government intended to repeal the Corn Production Act and to abolish the Agricultural Wages Board. The cause of this sudden policy change was the tumble worldwide in agricultural prices. The British government estimated that to continue guaranteed prices for corn would now cost it £20 million annually.

The vital role which the AWB and the statutory minimum wage had played in stimulating the organisation of farm workers in 1917-18 has already been stressed. A guaranteed wage had assured the Transport Union that these workers would be capable of maintaining the 6d weekly subscription, and so organisers had been sent into the countryside to agitate for an even better standard of living for farm employees. Now, however, in changed economic circumstances, the government eliminated the statutory minimum wage, which put the responsibility totally on the trade union to maintain wages henceforth.

The simultaneous abolition of the guaranteed price for corn meant that farmers would probably grow less of it in future and revert to pre-War patterns of pasture and stock raising, which would threaten employment even further. The abolition of the AWB was bitterly denounced by worker representatives. Thomas Johnson, secretary of the Irish Labour Party/Trade Union Congress warned that the decision would lead to friction and dispute (Irish Times, 10.6.21). An **Irish Times** 'source' commented that the attempt to deprive the agricultural labourer of his charter of liberty, which the Prime Minister, Lloyd George, referred to as the greatest of the reforms of his administrtion, "would add deplorably to the existing unrest" (ibid.). A.E. (George Russell) considered the government to be breaking faith with farmers and labourers alike, but the labourers had the greatest grievance (**Irish Homestead**, 18.6.21).

The Standing Committee of Cork Farmers' Union, on the other hand, unanimously welcomed the announcement, saying it would relieve the industry from "many harassing restrictions" (CE, 20.6.21). Thus, when the truce in the Anglo-Irish War was enforced on 11 July, the potential for conflict on the agricultural front was greater than ever. In summary, it is noted that, during the last eight months of the Anglo-Irish War, trade union branches in rural Cork suffered damage and setbacks from war and unemployment, but for the most part remained intact.

During the truce, the Dail government insisted as strongly as ever that the national interest could not suffer strikes and consequent strife in the countryside. It quickly transpired, however, that neither farmers nor labourers were willing to sacrifice their personal interests once military hostilities had been suspended.

On 27 July, a farm strike started in Aghada, the parish where the 'Red Guards' had held sway for a week the previous year. The issue was the rate of pay for the coming year, because parishes in that area, in contrast to most other parts of Cork, made the annual agreement in August rather than on Ladyday, 25 March. The strike was bitterly fought, with burnings and destruction of property occuring during the first week. The local ITGWU branch secretary then put notices in the **Examiner** condemning such action (CE, 4.8.21, 5.8.21). After three and a half weeks of strike the branch secretary appealed to the workers of Cork city and county for financial help, explaining that single men could keep going on dispute pay, but that married men with large families could not. In such a situation, even after the strike was settled, both farmers and employees nourished a sense of grievance at their losses.

The Red Flag also quickly made its re-appearance after the signing of the truce, indicating that militant trade unionism was again emerging. On 5 September labourers employed by Cork Harbour Commissioners took over the running of the port and raised a red flag over the Commissioner's Office. This seizure caused a great stir in the city and had reverberations in the county in the months that followed. On the morning that he was installed as the 'Chief Commissioner of the Port of Cork', Transport Union organiser, Bob Day, TC, was openly defiant. The **Examiner** reported him addressing the workers as:

> "Friends, comrades and Bolsheviks..."
>
> "He did not think there was any better title for them than Bolsheviks, for that word meant to him an anxiety that the bottom dog should go up and the top dog come down. While life was in him, his policy would always be to bring up the bottom dog and put the top dog down. When they raised their Red Flag people laughed at them and said that they were a pack of sillies. They had proved that whatever flag the people had faith in, the workers had faith in the Red Flag, and the Red Flag only" (CE, 7.9.21; see also CE, 6, 8, 10, 13, 15, 16.9.21).

The example was followed in the Whitechurch (Blarney) farm strike in November. A local union correspondent wrote "the Red Flag floats over the village and is nailed to the mast" (**Voice of Labour**, 26.11.21). The Whitechurch dispute also signals the start of direct IRA intervention and consequent attempts by both labourers and farmers to manipulate that army to their own advantage.

The strike started on 7 November 1921 when the local farmers notified a reduction of 7/6 on the 41/- wage for seven days. The reason given was that farm prices had fallen 48% from the previous year and the cost of living had dropped 26 1/2% (CE, 7.1.22).

The advantage was on the employers' side because November heralded the slack period on many farms. Accordingly, the labourers adapted forceful tactics. During the second week of the strike the roads leading from Cork city to Whitechurch were picketed. Breadvan and groceryvan drivers who were members of Transport Union were told not to deliver to farmers whose men were on strike. The two publicans in the village who were also farmers were prevented from selling beer to anyone. Grains for cattle feeding were held up. When that action proved insufficient to force a settlement, the forty farm workers on strike decided to hold up the large quantity of milk supplied to the city from Whitechurch farms (**Voice of Labour**, 10.12.21). On Monday 28 November the milk was held up by pickets, but the next morning the milk carts were guarded by armed men who proved to be IRA members under the command of a local farmer's son. The ITGWU newspaper commented: "Because a man of the farmer class was in control, he mobilised the Volunteers to do duty against the pickets!" One working man in the IRA who was called out at 6 am refused point blank to act against other workers when told the business involved. The Transport Union then complained to Cork HQ IRA about the army being used in that way, causing an immediate intervention from HQ which persuaded both sides to accept a Dail Arbitration Court.

While a farmer's son had exploited his position to use the IRA against the strikers, the Transport Union newspaper had then given prominent space to the story, and had written it in such terms as to embarrass the IRA and thus prevent a recurrence, or gain sympathy for the Union's position from the Dail. The IRA continued to intervene, however, mostly in favour of farmers.

That was the pattern in the prolonged Bartlemy (Fermoy) dispute. Labourers there demanded a £4 harvest bonus in July 1921. When it was refused, a four-week strike followed in August during which there were burnings of property (CE, 23.7.21; **Voice of Labour**, 19.11.21). Farmers responded by cutting off the milk supply to Transport Union members and announcing the intention to keep the supply cut off throughout the winter. The local ITGWU branch then informed head office that a sister of one of the Union labourers had fallen seriously ill and the doctor ordered that she get nothing but milk. Local farmers refused to supply it (**Voice of Labour**, 12.11.21). Eventually the Department of Labour Arbitration awarded £2 harvest bonus payable by 1 October, but by 21 October union members complained that most farmers still had not paid it (ibid., 22.10.21).

Then in November the employers counter-attacked by notifying a 25% reduction in wages from 27 November. The reduction was first imposed on the jobs where the three most active members of the union were employed, which sparked off another strike (ibid., 6.12.21). The IRA were then drafted into the area, with strikers claiming that local farmers in the IRA attempted to intimidate them nightly with bursts of rifle or shot-gun fire (ibid., 24.12.21). In January 1922 six of the strikers were arrested by the IRA, the union's only redress being to complain to the chief of the Republican Police (ibid., 11.2.22).

An equally protracted dispute began in Gurtroe (Youghal) on 22 November 1921. Farmers demanded a big reduction from 36/- to 25/- per week and the **Examiner** reported "that in consequence the Transport Workers were either called out or locked out" (CE, 25.11.21). The 80 strikers then, according to the report they sent to their Union's newspaper, "worried, harassed and hit [the employers] from every feasible angle" twenty four hours a day (**Voice of Labour**, 10.12.21). The Republican police were then introduced and, the strikers claimed, used against them (ibid.). The dispute dragged on for almost three months before arbitration was agreed, resulting in the old rate of pay being restored until 25 March.

Outside County Cork a similar pattern of bitter farm strikes, accompanied by agrarian crime, the re-emergence of the Red Flag, and IRA intervention, is recorded during the winter of 1921-2. At Christmas 1921 the **Irish Farmer**, organ of the IFU, warned that, if the strike tactics employed then were continued, the only solution for the farmers would be to "shut out all over Ireland the members of the union which countenances blackguardism and violence" (**Irish Farmer**, 24.12.21).

An examination of a dispute in County Limerick during that winter 1921-22 reveals the same pattern of events. A strike over a £4 harvest bonus began in Bulgaden (Kilmallock) on 9 November 1921. The creamery was forced to close down. The house of a farmer was entered a few nights later and his separator for making butter stolen, presumably to prevent him from processing the milk himself while the creamery was out of action. As a result, four ITGWU officials were arrested by the IRA and taken to an unknown destination. It was later claimed that a Transport Union man was tarred and feathered by the IRA during the dispute (CE, 19.12.21 at General Meeting ITGWU in January). In response to the arrests, the ITGWU declared Kilmallock creamery closed also. On Saturday 19 November 300 strikers and supporters paraded through Kilmallock carrying a red flag in protest at the arrests and in tribute to Tadg Barry, whose coffin was passing through by train that day from Ballykinlar to Cork (CE, 15.11.21, 22.11.21).

The dispute remained deadlocked for another month and a half but turned very serious at the end of December when large quantities of hay belonging to farmers in the district were maliciously set on fire and destroyed (ibid., 30.12.21). Martial law was then declared by Commandant Hennigan (East Limerick Brigade IRA) and Volunteers were drafted in from other areas to patrol and protect property. Despite the patrols, on January 26 it was reported that a few nights previously the walls of J. Connors in Ardvullen were knocked down, the entrance gates taken and electricity supply line to the house severed (ibid., 26.1.22). A return to work pending arbitration was agreed at the end of January. Martial law continued, however, and though the dispute appeared settled by arbitration at the start of March it had flared up again a week later, leading to the arrest of Dowling and McGrath, the top two Transport Union officials in the area (CE, 3.3.22, 8.3.22, 10.3.22).

Thus when annual 'county' agreements came up for renewal in the spring of 1922 farmers in Munster and Leinster were certain to press for a wage reduction, as they had been doing on a district basis since the previous autumn. The response of the ITGWU in its best organised counties, such as Dublin and Meath, would be important for its reputation in other regions. When the annual negotiations for Dublin and Meath broke down in March, 2,000 labourers in Dublin and 1,000 in Meath went on strike. A similar pattern of IRA intervention was recorded with a Transport Union official writing from Meath:

> "...Mr McCann of Meath has eight IRA fully armed guarding the blacklegs... Yesterday myself and two other representatives were held up for four hours by the IRA. There were about twelve men at the crossroads armed with revolvers and shotguns. In my twenty years experience of strikes I have not seen such a display of temper on the part of representatives of law and order. The pretext for this, I gathered, was that some men on strike went to a farm near Fodstown with a motor and ordered into it a man who was not in the Union..." (**Voice of Labour**, 18.3.22).

IRA intervention did not deter the strikers from obstructing the roads and the Dublin market, however, so that within days all of County Meath and all of County Dublin, with the exception of districts in the north of the county around Skerries, Lusk and Balbriggan, were successful in retaining the 1921 rates of pay. The ITGWU leadership in Dublin was jubilant at what it saw as a victory in difficult economic circumstances and declared: "After Meath, Cork next!" (**Voice of Labour**, 25.3.22).

This referred to the approach of Ladyday, 25 March, when annual agreements were traditionally made for most of County Cork. There had been disputes in several Cork districts during the winter of 1921-22, as seen above, but the extent of resistance to attempted reductions on 25 March would be taken on all sides in the County as the barometer of Transport Union strength.

When farmers in the districts adjacent to the city failed to attend a conference to discuss threatened reductions, all the farm labourers in the Liberties went on strike on 22 March 1922. Up to 800 men in the parishes of Lehenagh, Bishopstown, Ballincollig, St Mary's, Whitechurch, Blarney, Douglas and Riverstown were involved (CE, 22, 25, 28.3.22, **Voice of Labour**, 25.3.22). A few days later 100 men in Buttevant also struck, followed by the Shanballymore branch (**Voice of Labour**, 1.4.22). At the end of the first week the Douglas area and half of the men in St Mary's were settled at the previous year's rate. After two weeks of strike, matters took a serious turn on the night of 3 April 1922, when trees were cut down, trenches dug, and other obstacles erected to block all the roads leading into the city (CE, 5.4.22, **Voice of Labour**, 15.4.22). In this way the milk supply was held up. New efforts to find a settlement were prompted by such action and a week later Lehenagh and the remainder of the St Mary's branch were settled at the old rates (CE, 5.4.22). In Shanballymore the old rate was also retained, though in Buttevant a 2/- reduction on the previous rates was imposed. The struggle was longest in Ballincollig and Bishopstown, continuing for five weeks in the former and eight weeks in the latter (**Voice of Labour**, 22.4.22, 29.4.22. 20.5.22).

The results of these strikes in Cork were mixed. They were significant, however, in that they demonstrate that in many parts of the county, particularly within a ten mile radius of the city, trade union organisation was still formidable amongst farm labourers. They were still in a position to compel employers to pay the previous year's rates in several areas, and to keep reductions to a minimum in others. The rate of pay for the coming year was thus settled in most Cork districts prior to the outbreak of the Civil War on 28 June.

Even those not directly involved in the Civil War were numbed and horrified by the fratricidal strife. The deaths in tragic circumstances of national figures, whose political philosophy they might not even have shared, distracted people, at least temporarily, from their own sectional interests. The death of Michael Collins, in particular, was mourned by all social classes in County Cork. The atrocities committed by both sides at local level also aroused strong emotions leading to divisions, disillusionment and despair which affected all sectional movements. Rural trade union organisations suffered very badly.

The dislocation of economic life caused by the Civil War exacerbated the effects on employment of the world depression. Broken bridges, mined roads, and the destruction of communications systems disrupted work in the countryside while the difficulty of holding fairs and markets added to the farmer's problems. From the trade union viewpoint the cancellation of branch meetings and the hazards of travel meant that rural members fell into arrears with subscriptions, increasing the likelihood of their falling away completely from the branch.

For example, the Fermoy ITGWU branch reported in August 1922 that: "slackerism is rampant among the agricultural sections — the job is one for an organiser and his job is to get there" (**Voice of Labour**, 12.8.22).

Aghada, Doneraile and Killavullen branches all reported in October 1922 that farmers were "chipping away" at wage rates, but that members were unable to respond because of the Civil War (ibid., 14.10.22, 21.10.22).

It appears also that the 'mopping up' operations by the Free State Army were used as an opportunity to settle old scores in the agricultural sector. Thus, from Fermoy came the report that on Sunday 19 November a detachment of National troops, under the command of a local farmer's son, raided the Catholic church in Bartlemy. Four of the 'old guard' of the ITGWU were arrested. One man was released some days later but reported that, while in custody, he was charged with cutting the harness of a farmer's horse during the farm strike the previous year (ibid., 9.12.22).

In the Dail on 20 April 1923 the Minister for Defence was asked to state the reasons for the arrest of the Chairman, Secretary and four members of the Bishopstown ITGWU branch. General Mulcahy replied that the branch secretary had been arrested and sentenced by military court in connection with a bomb outrage in Bishopstown and that he was "making inquiries into the cases of the other men" (Dail Reports, Vol 3, col 313, 20.4.23). Two weeks later all were still in custody and Bob Day TD alleged in the Dail that "the general opinion in Cork is that the military have taken sides in a labour dispute which exists" in Bishopstown (ibid., col 604, 4.5.23).

By the spring of 1923 there was low morale and apathy in many rural trade union branches. Increasing unemployment made those who were working more conscious of the reserve labour pool in the countryside, with the result that some began to fear risking a strike. The decision on strike action was normally made by the vote of branch members, and at the start of 1923 rural branch secretaries of the ITGWU reported increasing cases of strike action being rejected (**Voice of Labour** 24.4.23).

There was increasing difficulty in maintaining influence over 'slackers' and non-union men, and the union now began to fume against them as being as much the enemy as the employer. In March 1923 the secretary of Buttevant branch wrote angrily that there had been 120 farm labourers in the branch the previous year, but after the union had secured a twelve-month agreement on wages and conditions "75 dastards stole from the ranks, leaving a remnant of 45 to fight this year's battle" (ibid., 10.3.23).

Because travel was difficult, some branch committees admitted to ITGWU Head Office that they had no interest in the scattered rural workers. At the beginning of March, in anticipation of the coming wage campaign, ITGWU Head Office circularized the 51 branches in Co. Cork to inquire about the position with regard to farm workers. Blarney branch replied that they were only concerned with the woollen mills and had little interest in farm workers, who were all unorganised in that area.

Head Office, however, insisted that a drive be made to restore organisation in rural Cork before Ladyday, 25 March. A remarkable recovery was made, which was indicated when many Cork branches were able to renew terms at the previous year's rates. Cork received encouragement in mid-March when the 'county' agreement of the previous year was retained in Meath without a strike, while in Dublin only 200 out of 2,000 farm workers were required to strike for the previous year's rate.

A strike started in Shanballymore, Co. Cork on 20 March 1923 and at the end of a week's picketing the previous year's rates of pay were restored until March 1924 (ibid., 24.3.23, 31.3.23). Douglas, Ballygarvan, Watergrasshill, Ballyhea, Knockraha, Carrigtwohill and Killeagh then settled at the previous year's rate (ibid., 31.3.23), while in St. Mary's and Lehenagh reductions were bargained down to 2/-, though farmers had demanded a 7/- reduction (ibid., 7.4.23, 14.4.23).

Thus, despite the difficulties of the Civil War and worsening economic depression, many farm labourers in Cork were still sufficiently organised in the spring of 1923 to maintain wage levels, though the employing farmers were trying their best to lower them. It would have been possible to rebuild from that base as the Civil War ended. However, three major farm strikes/lockouts occurred in 1923 in Athy, Ballingarry and Co. Waterford. These were the most prolonged and bitter farm strikes ever fought in Ireland, the outcome of which was to undermine confidence, throughout the country, in the maintenance of trade union organisation amongst farm workers.

A vital factor in the 1923 strikes, absent during the previous four years, was the role of stable government, military and police. The hold of the Free State Army was strengthening over most of the twenty six counties by January 1923. The government, accordingly, in contrast to previous years, was in a position to act as 'referee' in the farm strikes, to ensure that the rules were obeyed. From the government's viewpoint the rules implied — in addition to the protection of property — orderly picketing, the prevention of behaviour which could be interpreted as intimidation and, where necessary, the escorting of convoys.

The labourers' success, on the other hand, in achieving and maintaining wage increases was, as has been demonstrated, frequently due to the combination of trade union agitation with traditional agrarian violence. However much the trade union representative might repudiate the burning and destruction of property, these had played a part in frightening employing farmers into granting increases.

Indeed, the language used in the ITGWU official organ, **The Voice of Labour**, throughout 1922-3 could be interpreted as incitement. Kevin O'Higgins, Minister for Home Affairs, interpreted it in that way and commented in the Dail in 1923. His statement is worth quoting as an indication of what the government's attitude to rural union agitation would be in the months ahead:

> "Now I occasionally read a Labour journal, not regularly, but occasionally, and one particular journal strikes me from week to week as calculated to create anything but an atmosphere of security. Personally, if I were in the farming line, and if in the early spring I was laying my plans for the year, and if it were a question whether I would break a particular field or not, and if that journal were to fall into my hands occasionally, and if I took from it the general tone and outlook of organised labour in the country, I would reflect very seriously about whether I would break the field, because I would consider it was questionable whether I would reap what I sowed or not, whether I would have a disastrous strike that would leave my produce caught by the weather, and if not caught by the weather, and if I had cut it in safety and got it into stocks, whether there might not be some disastrous spontaneous combustion that would leave things equally bad..." (quoted in **Voice of Labour**, 13.1.23).

An incident which occurred in January 1923, near the beginning of the year-long Athy farm strike/lockout demonstrates the tone of language referred to by Mr. O'Higgins. When the 300 labourers on 90 farms in the Athy area had been out for a month, the secretary of the Athy ITGWU branch, Christy Supple, was arrested by the military and taken to Carlow barracks. When no charges had been preferred against him after several weeks, William O'Brien raised Supple's case in the Dail (Dail Reports, Vol 4, col 1579-88, 21.2.23). It was then revealed that Supple was to be charged in connection with a letter he had sent in his capacity as branch secretary to a Mr. Melville, a labourer who refused to strike. It read

> A chara,
>
> After careful consideration [by the Committee] I was directed to write to you to inform you to strike on Monday next and report to me. Failing to do this we will be compelled to take drastic action both against you and your employer, and do all in our power against him.
>
> Hoping that after this notice you will cease work.
>
> Yours faithfully,
>
> C.J. Supple 'Secretary'

Following the sending of the letter, Melville was fired at and wounded in the hand.

The ITGWU protested that the letter was drafted in exactly the same terms as hundreds of letters which were sent out from trade union offices and branch secretaries every day (**Voice of Labour**, 24.2.23). Deputy Wilson (Farmers' Party), on the other hand, declared that the word 'drastic action' was interpreted by farmers, rightly or wrongly, as burnings (Dail Reports, Vol 4, col 1581, 21.2.23).

The Athy dispute grew increasingly bitter. In January the Farmers Flying Column (FFC) made its appearance. It was alleged to have put up notices at night all over the district warning farmers who had not joined the lockout to do so and warning labourers to strike in accordance with trade union regulations. The Athy ITGWU branch claimed the FFC broke windows of cottages and threatened union officials with shooting and death (**Voice of Labour**, 13.1.23). Then up to ten haggards in the district were burned out. The union claimed it was the work of the FFC to intimidate farmers who wouldn't lock out their employees, while Kildare Farmers' Assocaition blamed the burnings on the labourers (Dail Reports, Vol 2, col 1584, 21.2.23; **Voice of Labour**, 3.3.23).

On 28 February a threshing engine owner was assaulted and his threshing machine and straw elevator broken at Bennetsbridge, Athy. Eight labourers who were picketing nearby were arrested and held in military custody for three months. The Transport Union paid compensation for the damage when their trial came up in May (Dail Reports, Vol 3, col 474-5, 2.5.23, col 2049, 19.6.23). Athy was a strong barley-growing area, but little was sown that year. According to newspaper reports at harvest time, the dispute was still in progress, and dragged on into the winter.

Another bitter dispute started in Kilmanagh and Ballyline (Ballingarry) in April 1923 when the labourers' claim for an increase on the 28/- wage was rejected. From the outset, a red flag was flown over Kilmanagh Workers' Hall. While the military and Civic Guards did not unduly interfere with the pickets at first, the workers were annoyed by the fact that all produce of the local creamery was transported under armed guard (**Voice of Labour**, 5.5.23).

At the beginning of June, however, the situation deteriorated when a fresh squad of infantry arrived in the district. On 12 June 1923 soldiers from this squad, under the command of an officer, pulled down the Red Flag, sprinkled it with petrol and burned it. The officer was reported as declaring there "was to be only one flag in Ireland and that he'd allow no Bolshevism" (ibid., 3.6.23). Three days later, the union claimed, the military searched the Transport Union Hall in Kilmanagh, and on leaving claimed that the place would be burned if further meetings were held there (ibid., 30.6.23).

The military then imposed their rule on the situation. On June 15 it was announced that no large pickets would be allowed, the maximum to be six men to each four miles of road. On 18 June a number of the strikers went to 'interview' a labourer who wasn't on strike. On the way back they were stopped by the military and lined up on both sides of the road. It was alleged that one man was then picked out, arrested, beaten on the face, and kicked while on the ground by a lieutenant (ibid., 30.6.23).

In July the dispute became much more widespread when 300 men in Ballingarry itself struck after employing farmers decided to impose a reduction of

8/- per week. Women and girls were involved in the picketing thenceforth. Farmers were prevented from selling cattle at both Kilkenny and Callan fairs in September, while the advent of the harvest season raised stakes even higher. Like the Athy dispute, the Ballingarry one dragged on into November.

Both of those strikes, however, were surpassed in ferocity by the Co. Waterford dispute. Waterford labourers had not been as well organised as those in Dublin, Meath and Kildare before 1921, but in 1922 the county rate was preserved intact when it had broken down in most other counties. Thus in 1923 organised farm workers in the county were in a better position than those in most other counties, with the exception of Dublin and Meath, to resist reductions. Because the Waterford strike was to have such significance for farm workers all over the country it is worthy of close attention.

When employing farmers demanded a 6/6 to 8/- reduction on a 35/- wage for six days, 1,500 labourers throughout the county struck on 17 May. The first phase of the strike was a period of union aggression and confidence. The press reported that picketing all over the affected area prevented the movement of goods to the city and to creameries.   Following appeals from the union, sympathetic action was taken by dockers, railwaymen, shop assistants, carters, creamery workers, domestic servants and factory workers, who all refused to assist the farmers involved (E. O'Connor, **Agrarian Unrest and the Labour Movement in Co. Waterford, 1917-23**, *Saothar vi*, (1980), p.48).

Where the farm workers did not get support, tough tactics were adopted. In Kilmeaden, where the creamery workers passed union pickets, a raid on the plant sabotaged machinery (ibid., and **Munster Express**, 2.6.23). After a few days of strike the army intervened against the pickets to keep routes open to traffic from the farms. By the second week, farmers had resorted to moving their supplies in convoy under military protection.   On May 29 a convoy was ambushed by rifle and revolver fire, the officer in command being slightly wounded (ibid., 2.6.23).

This heralded the second phase of the strike as a Special Infantry Corps comprising 250 men arrived from Dublin on 1 June, about the same time that they took over in Ballingarry. The Specials provided escorts for all convoys as intermittent sniping continued, and conducted arms and ammunition searches (ibid., 30.6.23). By the end of June the Specials were 600 strong and on 4 July a curfew was imposed in all of East Waterford, bar the city, and martial law declared in the curfew zones. Anyone out of doors without a permit between 11.00 pm and 5.30 am was to be arrested.

Despite these measures, however, labourers continued to mount illegal operations. The Specials replied with raids on Union rooms, confiscation of flags and emblems, and the impounding of records and documentation. Direct confrontation with the strikers became more frequent. On 30 June John Butler, Labour TD, and six others were arrested and detained in Dungarvan Barracks for half an hour for refusing to disperse large crowds of workers who had assembled for a union meeting in Grattan Square. In Fenor nine pickets were arrested and tried by special court, after the military claimed to have found a shotgun in a nearby labourer's cottage. On 19 July Civic Guards, backed up by the Specials, baton-charged a crowd in Ballybricken who were protesting against the movement of pigs into the city for slaughter. Emmet O'Connor comments that the dispute was "escalating into a miniature civil war" (O'Connor p.50).

Despite the efforts of the Specials, labourers continued to destroy haggards, damage machinery, spike meadows, break down gates and gate posts, and maim and drive off cattle. With the advent of harvest, farmers began to return the terror of the labourers. A group styled the "White Guards" raided and burned the cottages of union activists (Dail Reports, Vol 5, col 432, 31.10.23), while the secretary of the Strike Committee claimed that "carloads of vigilantes toured the countryside, waylaying strikers and pistol-whipping them" (O'Connor, p.53). James Baird, the ITGWU organiser in the region, was arrested and interned on 6 September under the Public Safety Act, 1923 for "encouraging the commission of arson" (Dail Reports, Vol 5, col 7, 25.9.23)..

By October ITGWU Head Office was desperately looking for a solution. But the Waterford Farmers' Association (WFA) rejected the offer made by the Minister for Agriculture on behalf of the ITGWU. The WFU declared that it was opposed to the union and would only negotiate with the men directly. This attitude reflected the position of the Farmers' Party candidates during the General Election in August when they declared themselves to be "the friends of honest workers but opposed to Bolshevism" (O'Connor, p.52).

In December the ITGWU executive decided it could no longer carry the burden of £1,500 per week dispute pay in Waterford and called off the strike. The union spent £128,724 in strike pay in 1923, compared to £33,139 the previous year. The biggest portion of that 1923 expenditure was on the prolonged farm strikes in Athy, Ballingarry and Waterford.

The repercussions of the collapse of those strikes was profound for farm labourers throughout Munster and Leinster. When rates of pay and working conditions came up for review in 1924, in most counties, including Cork, the farm employees were no longer in a position to negotiate. The ITGWU **Annual Report** 1924 recorded "successful negotiations" for the farm workers in Meath, Dublin and Wicklow, but there was no mention of any other area (p.9). By 1927 the union admitted that the farm workers had become almost entirely unorganised (ibid., 1927, p.18).

In addition, in the aftermath of the Waterford dispute, those on strike were taken back at their employers' discretion, the more militant workers being victimised in many instances (**Voice of Labour**, 22.12.23). It seems likely, given the rampant unemployment which created a large reserve pool in the countryside, that some of the more militant labourers in other counties were also victimised in 1924 when it became clear that Union support was no longer forthcoming.

There is evidence too that the Gardai frowned on attempts at reorganisation by rural labourers in 1924. Because organised farm workers appeared to be associated with violence and unrest, the authorities were apprehensive in the post-Civil War atmosphere about any recurrence of such activities. Thus, in October 1924, the Minister for Justice was asked in the Dail to explain why a Garda Sergeant at Meelin, North Cork, had pulled down a poster calling for a meeting of the 'Independent Landless League' on 5 October 1924 at Gooseberry Hill, Meelin. Kevin O'Higgins replied that the meeting was called for 3.00 pm and the Sergeant wanted to attend the meeting. When no one had arrived by 3.30 pm he felt he should remove the notice. This ministerial reply drew derisive rejoinders from other Deputies, who felt that there was more to the issue than what the Minister disclosed (Dail Debates, Vol 9, col 15-6, 22.10.24).

As a conclusion to the study of the 1918-23 period, it is worthwhile to review the role of the rural branch secretary. In the unprecedented advance of trade unionism in rural Ireland during those years the role of branch secretary was a crucial one. It was he who had initially to hold together a few new converts after a flying visit from a union organiser. The doctrines and tactics of the One Big Union were new to the rural worker and the task of overcoming his suspicions had to be undertaken. Those first branch members in the parish were vulnerable in the workplace to the employer's hostility to trade unionism, because the nature of farm work implied frequent solitary labour and regular personal encounters with the employer.

In such circumstances, the secretary had to bolster any flagging morale among recent converts, while simultaneously trying to win new recruits. He frequently had to chase members for the weekly 6d subscription and for arrears. His, too, was the difficult task of confronting the farmer who refused to pay the union rate, or was in breach of an agreement. That was particularly the case in 1918-19, before farmers themselves became widely organised, thus facilitating more centralised bargaining. The effort and determination (or lack of them) of the branch secretary had a big bearing on the health and growth of the branch. A portrait of the secretary of one small Cork County branch illustrates this.

Maurice O'Regan, Secretary of the Bartlemy (Fermoy) branch in 1920-1, was more adept at writing to the newspapers than most, so that it is possible to trace the rise and fall of his branch. Maurice combined the position of IRA Flying Column section leader with that of union branch secretary up to the truce of July 1921. The language of the notices he put in the **Examiner** during that period was more blunt than that used by other secretaries. Thus, for example, he warned members in arrears that, unless their cards were cleared up immediately, they would be suspended from membership of the union "and treated as blacklegs" (CE, 14.5.21).

He led the bitter farm strike in Bartlemy in August 1921, when the burnings of property occurred and farmers responded by cutting off the milk supply to Transport Union members. The Red Flag was raised in the village and O'Regan was enthusiastic in extolling its virtues. He composed a song, the first verse of which was

> "The farmers viewed with great alarm
> The flag of Red that the Transport flew;
> There was consternation on every farm,
> From the hilltops of Moranig to the graveyard of Gortrue."
> (Voice of Labour, 19.11.21).

At the end of 1921, in order to make rural organisation more effective and combat unemployment, the Transport Union devised the Big Branch scheme. All the branches in a district would amalgamate, with each having two representatives on the district committee, and a paid secretary to look after the district. Thus, in Cork, the Big Branches were centred in Fermoy, Mallow, Macroom, and Midleton. Maurice O'Regan was promoted to the position of district secretary in Fermoy (ibid., 25.5.22). It was difficult to overcome parochialism and convince some branches of the merits of the scheme, but by June 1922 six small branches had joined with Fermoy (ibid., 20.5.22).

O'Regan was relentless in chasing up the demands of members and took it as a compliment when farmer Jeffrey of Fermoy described him as "the greatest scoundrel that ever came into the place" (ibid., 24.6.22).

The Civil War had a shattering effect on the Fermoy area and by February 1923 O'Regan was reporting hunger, despondency, cynicism and bitterness among the membership. Those outside the union, he said, who thought it too much to pay a 'tanner' a week, were "slandering the union and its officials in the pub every night". He struggled on, however. During the spring of 1923 farmers all round Fermoy imposed reductions on those labourers not in the union. However, when a strong farmer in the area tried to enforce reductions on his four men, who were members of the union, O'Regan led the four in a strike in May. He rebuked the slackers—

> "only four, alone, all alone in a district reeking with non-unionism and scabbery and consequent slavery, taking up the challenge of this unscrupulous boss who would take the bread out of their childen's mouths, whilst he has thousands of pounds rotting in the banks..." (ibid., 16.6.23).

The split with Jim Larkin in June 1923 added to the problems at local level, with O'Regan declaring that, as one who had always admired Larkin, he could not now find words strong enough to condemn his actions (ibid., 30.6.23). Thus, instead of support for the four-man strike, O'Regan reported in July that the wicked rumours about the union were getting worse. First, it was said that the Chairman and the Committee were drinking all the money, another time that the Union had decided to burn motor lorries, then that the union refused to pay mortality benefit to someone, and then that the officials were reaping all the benefits in fat salaries (ibid., 14.7.23). O'Regan himself was accused of drawing a fat salary and having the cheek to draw the dole at the same time. He revealed that all he was getting from the Union for all his trouble was 4/- per week which, added to the dole, made 19/- (ibid.).

Despite the detractors, he battled on with the four strikers, winning out after two months, when farmer O'Brien restored the old rate of pay (ibid., 4.8.23). O'Regan's efforts were not in vain as, two weeks after the four-man strike ended, he was appointed ITGWU organiser for Galway, where the pickings, no doubt, were more than 4/- per week.

His small strike coincided with the three big ones in Athy, Ballingarry and Waterford. The fate of trade unions in rural Cork also depended on the outcome in those areas. When the strikes collapsed there, morale in Cork faded also.

THE WAR OF LABOUR

AT a Meeting of the Agricultural Labourers' Section of the Irish Transport and General Workers' Union, Fermoy Branch, the following demands were made:— 30s. a week, a house free, ½ an acre of garden, seeded, tilled and manured; a quart of new milk per day, and 30 cwt. of coal a year; 6 days' work of 9 hours per day. One shilling per hour overtime. No settlement to be made without communicating with Union Secretary. Not to work with non-Union men. To work for no other farmer except Employer, except when casual labour is unobtainable. To follow only Employer's Reaper and Binder. When taking place of casual labourers in the case already stated, to work for 5s. a day and nothing less. No distinction at table. Not to take up a position which another member is negotiating for. A living wage for Women and Girls. 2553

From Cork Examiner, 22.2.1919

Strike Scenes At Celbridge

ABOVE: Police escort for Lord Carew, while cutting corn at Celbridge.
BELOW: Farm strikers gathered around their meeting hall at Celbridge.

From Irish Press, 27.8.1946

chapter five

The Workers' Union Of Ireland And Federation Of Rural Workers 1944-48

During the late 1920s and 1930s little effort was made to revive trade unionism among farm workers. The issue was discussed regularly at ITGWU Conferences and by the ITUC, and while sympathy was always expressed, the constant conclusion was that it would not be possible to re-organise them at that particular time (**Annual Reports**, ITGWU and ITUC 1928-40, passim).

In the laissez-faire situation after 1923 the pay and working conditions of many farm workers deteriorated to such an extent that government intervention to fix a minimum wage became necessary in 1936. The inspectors of the new wage fixing body — the Agricultural Wages Board — recovered arrears and attempted to ensure that the minimum wage was being paid. The developments are discussed in detail in Chapter 6 below. This chapter highlights the fact that, after six years of AWB intervention, discontent among labourers gave rise to renewed trade union agitation.

The WUI began the task of re-organisation in 1943, and in 1946 that Union was instrumental in the foundation of a new organisation to cater for farm workers, the Federation of Rural Workers (FRW). As has been emphasised above, any advance towards combined action by agricultural labourers is significant because they were so notoriously difficult to organise. Therefore, close attention to the development of the farm workers' union during the 1940s is justified.

The fact that the farm strikes and activities of that period have not been documented by historians makes it necessary to present a narrative. Several points of interest emerge from a study of the strikes. The main issue involved was the demand for a weekly half-holdiay and a week's annual holidays with pay. That such a bitter struggle was waged, with intimidation, police intervention, and agrarian violence, testifies to the neglect felt by farm labourers. They had been excluded from the *Conditions of Employment Act, 1936* and the *Holidays (Employees) Act, 1939*, which granted those conditions to most other categories of worker. Indeed, when the farm workers were in dispute for one week's holiday, many other sections of the workforce were carrying on a campaign for *two* weeks' annual leave. The average hours of work per week in the industrial and services sectors were 44 during the early 1940s, but were still 54 in agriculture.

Another significant point concerning the farm strikes of the 40s is that they were made the focus of a red scare. The North Kildare farm strike, August-September 1946, was the occasion of a bitter onslaught against the labourer's union by the 'Catholic' newspaper, **The Standard**. Since that newspaper was sold at church gates around the country on Sundays, it was influential, at least to some degree, in forming public opinion. To be branded a communist in Ireland in the hysterical 'Iron Curtain' era of 1946-7 was a serious matter. Consequently, the task of organising farm labourers became more difficult for the FRW following the **Standard**'s allegations of communism against the union.

The altered economic conditions of World War II were conducive towards the combination of farm workers, as had been the pattern during World War I. Compulsory tillage orders meant there was an increased demand for agricultural workers, thus mitigating the problem of rural unemployment and surplus labour. At the same time, discontent was widespread because inflation caused rising prices, which were not matched with wage increases. Table 12 indicates the change in the cost of living 1939-44.

Table 12. Cost Of Living Increase 1939-44

Mid-August	Figure	Amount Required To Purchase Goods Valued at 20/- at mid-August, 1939
1939	173	20/-
1940	206	23/9 1/2d
1941	228	26/4 1/2d
1942	250	28/11
1943	284	32/10
1944	296	34/2

From Statistics published by Department of Industry And Commerce, Contained in ITGWU **Annual Report**, 1945

An extra 14/2 was required in August 1944 to purchase the same amount of goods as in 1939. However, the four increases granted by the AWB during the same period amounted to 13/-, which did not keep up with the cost of living, while the working week was still 54 hours. Agricultural wages increased from £1.13s. at top rate in 1939 to £2.6s. in 1944 (Memoranda published by AWB, 1939-44, available from Department of Labour, Davitt House, Waterloo Road, Dublin 4).

It was against such a background that Jim Larkin and his son, Jim Jnr. or 'Young Jim', began to organise in Co. Dublin in 1943. It was precisely 30 years since Larkin had held his first meetings for farm labourers in the villages of Co. Dublin in the months before the lockout (Chapter 2).

Organising work continued during spring 1944 and written reports survive of meetings held at Clondalkin on 21 April 1944 and Crumlin on 7 May 1944.* In the early summer of 1944 the organising drive extended to Wicklow,

---

* Manuscripts on the WUI and early years of the FRW in the possession of Mr. Patrick Murphy (President of the FRW until it merged with WUI in 1979 to form the FWUI). Manuscript held at Head Office, FWUI, 29 Parnell Square, Dublin 1. Mr. Murphy kindly gave me copies from the file. Henceforth referred to as **MSS, PM, FRW**.

Kildare and Meath, the slogan adopted being, "Speed the plough — pay the Ploughman" (MSS PM FRW, document entitled **F.R.W Formation and Development**). A test of WUI strength among farm workers came at harvest time, 1944. Strike notice was served on the employing farmers of Co. Dublin by the union on 4 August 1944, demanding an increase of 12/- on the £2 6s. rate, a reduction in the working week from 54 to 48 hours, which implied a weekly half-holiday, payment for overtime, and payment for either church or public holidays. Jim Larkin told an **Irish Times** reporter that 90% of the 5,000 Co. Dublin labourers were organised (IT, 5.8.1944, 7.8.1944). Even if that claim was exaggerated, the events which followed indicated union strength, as many farmers signed an agreement, and prolonged strike action was undertaken against an employer of over 30 farm labourers.

The **Irish Times** carried a long editorial on the strike threat, a few days after the demands were served, which gives a valuable insight into the labourers' position.

Though critical of Larkin's methods, it continued:

"...At the same time we must confess ourselves in sympathy with the farm labourers. They are, perhaps, the most important body of people in the entire country, except the farmers themselves; and they are almost certainly the worst paid. It is not enough to answer that they are fed for the most part by their employers. Their wives and children are not so fed; rent must be paid; most of the expenses that the city worker, with a larger income, incurs must be met also by the farm labourer on his comparatively low wage. When one considers the conditions of the farm labourer, indeed, it is hardly necessary to demand any further explanation for the 'flight from the land' which has received so much publicity in the past twenty years...

"The agricultural labourer deserves a better time — which by practical interpretation means more money, a better house, and at least such amenities as are enjoyed by the comparable workers in the city. Hitherto the men on the land have not employed the weapon of strike action, and we sincerely hope that their tens of thousands will never reach the point of coming out, whether in conditions of peace or war, but they have more excuse for it than most people and their quietness in the past is a tribute to them..." (Irish Times, 8.8.1944).

The criticism of Larkin in the editorial was that the **Irish Times** believed him to be playing "union politics" in the hope that, if the strike weapon succeeded in Co. Dublin, the farm labourers of the other twenty five counties "will come with a rush into the fold" (ibid.).

Larkin replied immediately with an equally long letter. While he expressed appreciation of the publicity given to the question, he resented the charge of union politics, declaring that the organisation of farm labourers was not a pleasant or easy task for any trade union, and that for his union there was nothing to be gained from it except a great deal of hard work (ibid., 10.8.44).

An immediate obstacle to the labourers' demands was that there was no organised body of farmers who could deal with the matter, and up to 2,000 employing farmers in Co. Dublin were involved. However, prominent farmers promised an adjustment of working conditions as soon as *employers* were organised, and immediately set about establishing such an organisation. The WUI suspended strike action temporarily on that assurance, and the mass demonstration planned for Dublin city centre on Sunday 20 August was postponed (ibid., 17.8.44, 21.8.44).

The Dublin Agriculturalists' Association was formed and the dispute partially settled with the signing of an agreement between the Association and the WUI on 7 September 1944 (ibid. 8.9.44). In addition, the Association recommended all Dublin farmers to accept the terms, whether they were members of the Association or not. The agreement gave an increase of 4/- for men, 2/- for youths, a 50-hour week, which meant a weekly half-day, and a full day's holiday with pay on each church holiday and public holiday. There was to be payment of time-and-a-quarter for any hours worked over 50, and payment for casuals other than those engaged in threshings was to be 10/- for a nine-hour day where work was less than the normal 5 1/2 days.

One prominent employer refused to accept the terms and a strike followed on his farm. That strike is worthy of attention because it heralded the return of farm strikes to Ireland, and because it illustrates the opposing perspectives at the time.

Patrick Belton farmed over 400 acres at Killiney. In 1944 he had 300 acres of tillage, and 130 to 140 first class dairy cows which supplied 200 gallons of milk to the city daily, according to his own calculations. He also had another farm at Drumcondra. Thirty male labourers were employed on the Killiney farm. On 9 October 1944, twenty-five of these workers plus twelve girls, aged 15-17, employed as potato pickers, went on strike when the pay increase and the half-day were refused (ibid., 13.10.1944, 23.10.1944). The response was the placing of large advertisements in the daily newspapers calling a meeting of farmers to form a new association, and also calling for government protection from the "destroyers of food". As a result, the National Agricultural Association was formed and a full-time organiser appointed (ibid. 17, 23, 26.10.1944).

When the dispute was two and a half weeks in progress, the employer claimed the strike was over, but the WUI insisted that up to 30 male and female workers were still affected. In a letter to the **Irish Times**, Patrick Belton ignored the pickets and declared: "My farm at Killiney is fully staffed, and I have no room for any more workers... All my regular staff at Killiney have returned to work with the exception of three... The talk of 20 or 30 hands still on strike here is pure fiction" (ibid., 1.11.44). The WUI then tried to prevent his produce from being sold in the Dublin market, which led to five members of the union being detained in the Bridewell, following a demonstration against a stall-holder who handled produce from the Killiney farm (ibid., 4.11.1944).

There was clearly a wide gap in communication in the dispute, which was seen in widely divergent terms. None of the newspaper advertisements made any reference to the half-day and public holidays, which were central issues from the workers' viewpoint. Eventually, the employer concerned claimed the strike occurred in the first place because the wages he paid were too *high*, and he placed a large box advertisement with the challenge that he would back the accuracy of his statement with £100, provided "Deputy Larkin, who led the strike, backs his statement with a similar amount, the loser to hand over his £100 as a bonus to my farm workers" (ibid.,11.11.1944).

In the autumn of 1944, Sean Dunne became Secretary of the Agricultural workers' section of the WUI. As he played a leading part in the early years of the FRW, his background is of interest. Born in Waterford in 1919, he was educated at Mount Sion Christian Brothers there. At the age of 16 he became involved in the Labour and Republican movements. He joined the WUI in 1936 and led the Hunger Marches of 1937. He spent two years in jail for republican activities, and on his release returned to work for the WUI. An admirer wrote in 1947 that it was impossible to spend even a short time in his company without realizing how "Larkin and the spirit of Larkinism has gripped his imagination and guided his actions" (**Irish People**, official organ of the Irish Labour Party, 27.9.47). In 1948 he was elected TD for Dublin County.

Throughout 1945 the WUI continued to make individual agreements with employing farmers in Co. Dublin, while intensive organisation work was carried on in counties Kildare, Meath and Wicklow. Union records contain a report on a meeting at Athy Town Hall held on 28 August 1945, addressed by Sean Dunne, among others. Athy had been the scene of one of the longest and most bitter farm strikes in Ireland during 1923 and the audience was reminded of this. Senator Michael Smyth "recalled the struggles of 25 years ago when the men of south Kildare stood fast together against the might of the employers" (MSS PM FRW, **Kildare Farm Workers**, 20.8.1945).

On the same day, a meeting was held at Kilkea Cross, South Kildare, where, according to the report, Sean Dunne stated that the practice of reducing wages in the late winter and early spring, which had grown up in the Kilkea area was unknown in Co. Dublin and would not be tolerated by the workers there. The report noted further that the Kilkea branch was already 120 strong, made up largely of employees on "what is said to be the largest tillage farm in these islands, an expanse of 1,800 acres" (ibid.).

By the autumn of 1945, the peculiar nature of the task of organising farm labourers had brought to bear on the Larkins and Dunne the realization that this class of workers required a separate union specially adapted to meet their needs (MSS PM FRW, **Formation and Development**). Accordingly, early in 1946 the WUI requested the ITUC to consider the possibility of organising rural workers throughout the country. A sub-committee of the National Executive of Congress was appointed to undertake the preliminary work. It consisted of:

Gilbert Lynch	ATGWU (President, ITUC)
Jim Larkin Jnr.	TD, WUI
P.J. Cairns	Post Office Workers' Union
Louie Bennett	Irish Women Workers' Union

Ruaidhrí Roberts   Secretary
Thomas Johnson   Former leader of the Labour Party
(MSS PM FRW **Formation of the F.R.W.**)

Other unions, notably the ITGWU, were not involved in the sub-committee because of the split in the trade union movement in 1945 following the resurgence of the Larkin-O'Brien feud in 1943 (see, for example, Lyons, p.678-680). The ITGWU, and other Irish-based unions broke with the ITUC and set up the Congress of Irish Unions (CIU). The Transport Union once more considered the question of re-organising farm workers at its annual conference in June 1946, but acting Vice-President John Conroy advised against "indiscriminate organisation": "Take the case of the agricultural workers for instance. If they were to organise such workers in one area they could not logically decline to accept them in other localities" (ITGWU **Annual Report** 1946, p.52). Accordingly, the decision was taken not to attempt organisation.

In the meantime, the ITUC sub-committee discussed the difficulties of rural organisation at a conference of interested persons on St. Patrick's Day 1946. Arising out of the discussion it was decided that the new union should have a *county* basis with each county associated in a federation framework. Provisional proposals, policy guidelines and draft rules were approved that St. Patrick's Day, and a new union, styled the Federation of Rural Workers would be launched in May (MSS PM FRW, ibid. See also File 493T, Registry of Friendly Societies, 13 Hume Street, Dublin 2).

Much drama intervened between March and May, however, and matters were further complicated by the stirrings of a nascent union for farm workers in competition with the WUI–FRW. It was titled the National Union of Agricultural Workers (NUAW). Its general secretary was T. J. Langan of Finglas, who had been Organising Secretary of the Agricultural Section, WUI, in 1944 prior to Sean Dunne. During 1945 Langan had concentrated on organising dairy workers only and, at the beginning of 1946, the nascent NUAW had negotiated with the County Dublin Dairymen for wage increases for milkers (MSS PM FRW, **Letter Jim Larkin to Dr. Ryan**, Minister for Agriculture, 13.4.46; **Irish Times**, 27.3.46).

Because of the existence of the two rival organisations, the NUAW was only half recognised by employers, a certain amount of confusion was generated in the lead up to the big Co. Dublin farm strikes of March-April 1946. On 25 March, the WUI served strike notice on the National Agricultural Assocation for 2,000 Co. Dublin members. The demand was for an increase of 14/-, a 48 hour week, one week's annual holiday, time and a half for overtime, 15/- a day casual rate and a harvest bonus. The strike notice was to expire four days later on Thursday, 28 March. Meanwhile the NUAW served strike notice on the same day on behalf of 1,000 workers, but it was not to expire until the following Sunday, 1 April, three days after the expiry of the WUI notice (**Irish Times**, 26.3.46). Confusion was created as, on the day before the WUI strike started,

Langan was busy telling the **Irish Times** that there would be no strike action until after the following Sunday (ibid., 27.3.46).

About 1,000 WUI labourers struck on 28 March with 300 farms being affected, while a further 200 workers joined the strike next day. The labourers' strategy was to cut off supplies to the Dublin vegetable market. Farms and roads leading to the city were picketed, and on Friday, the busy market-day, lorry- and cartloads of vegetables headed for the market were held up and some overturned. In some areas broken glass and barbed wire was spread across the road to hold up or puncture lorries (CE, 29, 30.3.46; **Irish Times**, 30.3.46). As a result vegetable deliveries to Dublin market were reduced by half. The entrance to the market was also picketed so that even some of those commodities that were delivered remained unsold. On Saturday morning about 100 strikers entered the market, but left when told by the Gardai and market superintendent that they could not picket inside. A few loads of cabbage which arrived from Finglas escorted by detectives were upset by the pickets and attempts were made to remove the lynchpins from the axles of farm carts (ibid., 1.4.46).

On Saturday afternoon, a conference was held at the Department of Industry and Commerce between the WUI and National Agricultural Association (NAA) at which settlement terms were worked out. An increase of 9/- on the AWB minimum and 5/- over the September 1944 settlement was granted, bringing the new minimum rates to 55/- near the city and 50/- in more outlying parts of the county. The principle of a 48-hour working week was accepted. Most important of all was that in the negotiations which followed the return to work the principle of one week's holidays with pay was granted, in addition to the guarantee of church or bank holidays free (ibid.).

The significance of this settlement was twofold. The WUI had now largely satisfied the demands of Co. Dublin members for the moment, which implied that the new union it proposed to sponsor could concentrate on achieving similar demands for the other twenty-five counties. Furthermore, the fact that the Dublin labourers had got the week's holidays would quickly become known to farm workers in those other counties, raising their expectations of similar conditions. Indeed, within two weeks of the Dublin settlement, Jim Larkin had written to the Minister for Agriculture, setting out in detail the significance of the Dublin agreement and urging a similar adjustment for the other twenty-five counties "to prevent any untoward movement" (MSS PM FRW, ibid.).

On the day the WUI strike ended, that of the NUAW began. T.J. Langan explained to a general meeting of members the efforts that had been made to induce the WUI to take joint action, but said every offer of theirs in that connection had been turned down. M.J. Brady, 'President' of the union, said he was "puzzled by the attitude of the WUI in refusing joint action" (**Irish Times**, 1.4.46). Jim Larkin, however, was openly dismissive of the other organisation, as his reference to it in a letter to the Minister for Agriculture indicates:

> "There was a group running round the country, who were alleged to be members of a union, of which one Langan claims to be general secretary, and a man named Brady, formerly a member of our Agricultural section, general organiser. They tried to create a certain amount of agitation by the issue of gross mis-statements which were published by the papers. Their union is registered but not licenced to negotiate..." (MSS PM FRW, ibid.).

The NUAW strike was not successful for several reasons. Because it started on the very day the WUI members returned to work, the confusion diminished the impact of the second strike. Secondly, since this new union was registered, but not licenced to negotiate, the Guards visited farms on the first day of strike action, informing the men that the new strike was illegal. In addition, while picketing by 800 men of the 200 farms affected took place, it did not appear to be forceful, though a Garda Superintendent did report that in Finglas and the north Dublin district generally, the Guards were on duty most of the night because of the strike (**Irish Times**, 1, 2, 3, 4, 5, 6, April 1946). Finally, the NUAW strike was less successful because many of the farmers who made agreements with this new union offered terms similar to those negotiated by the WUI, an outcome which did not really enhance the prestige of the NUAW (ibid.). The NUAW ceased to exist in 1947 (file 491T, Registry of Friendly Societies).

After the Dublin strikes, plans to launch the FRW went ahead, and in May 1946 the sub-committee of the National Executive, ITUC, formally constituted themselves as the nucleus of the new FRW. Rules were adopted on 21 June 1946, and the Provisional Executive appointed until a special conference in October. It comprised:

President	Jim Larkin Jnr. TD
Vice-President	John Duignan
Treasurer	P.J. Cairns, Post Office Workers' Union
Trustees	Thomas Johnson, Senator Michael Smyth
	Richard McCeann
Members	Gilbert Lynch, E.P. Harte, Louie Bennett,
	John Sherlock, George Pollock
Provisional Organising Secretary	Sean Dunne

Loans and grants were made available by several unions affiliated to the ITUC and on 1 August the FRW was issued a certificate of registration (ibid.). At the beginning of July about 4,000 members of the WUI in counties Dublin, Meath and Kildare transferred to the FRW. A letter, signed by Jim Larkin, to all members of the Farm and Road Workers' Section of the WUI, urging them to join the new union is contained in FRW files (ibid., **Letter from J. Larkin to members Farm and Road Workers Section**, c28.6.46). Organisation work was then extended to other counties, such as Cork and Tipperary.

The FRW had a stormy beginning. On 1 August strike action began on North Kildare farms. It proved to be the most bitter rural dispute of the decade. It quickly assumed national significance, because the North Kildare labourers were demanding the half-day and week's holidays recently guaranteed in Co. Dublin. If granted in Kildare, those contributing to the strike fund from Co. Cork and other counties would demand the same.

Kildare Farmers Association, recently re-organised, decided unanimously to resist the FRW demands, and "defeat strike action". It called for a government tribunal to investigate prices and wages in agriculture so that farmers could be put in a position to pay (**Irish Times**, 30.7.1946). Up to 600 workers struck on 1 August in the Maynooth, Clane and Celbridge districts and issued a statement declaring that, since their claim was "supported by every principle of justice and humanity", they would not be defeated (ibid., 3.8.46). There was intense picketing on the first day of the strike and that night it was alleged that hay which had been saved in cocks on seven farms was pulled down and strewn around the fields. The next night, it was claimed, cattle were put into fields of corn on two farms (ibid. 5.8.46; **The Standard**, 30.8.46).

Several employers claimed their men were being intimidated into striking. Lord Carew of Castletown, Celbridge, a leading spokesman for the farmers, wrote in a letter to the **Irish Times** that his men told him they were "perfectly happy with rates of pay and conditions", but that they were forced to go on strike (**Irish Times**, 3.8.46). E.J. Dease of Celbridge claimed that his five workers had always been happy with his father and himself, but that the men were out with his "permission", as "trying to work with pickets was putting them in an intolerable position" (ibid., 7.8.46). A Dublin reader responded in the **Irish Times** with the comment: "Thousands of slaves in America were devoted to their masters and opposed abolition... But slavery went; as all enforced low standards of life must go, because a democracy cannot afford them" (ibid., 9.8.46).

A few days after his letter to the newspaper, Lord Carew was forced to lock the gates of Castletown Demesne to prevent what he called "acts of vandalism" (ibid., 15.8.46). Fifty to sixty extra Gardai were drafted into the area at that stage to patrol farms and keep surveillance on strikers. Several individual settlements were reported during the first week, though Sean Dunne reported 500 men still out at the end of a week. Further individual settlements saw the number of strikes reduced to 200 by mid-August.

When conferences convened by the Department of Industry and Commerce on 17, 21, and 23 August ended without settlement, the struggle escalated into what the newspapers called an "agricultural civil war" (ibid., 29.8.46). With the harvest in danger, the employers decided to carry on harvesting operations with the help of neighbours and the organisation of 'Flying Columns' of farmers from other areas to assist at weekends. The revival of language such as 'Flying Columns' indicated that the 1923 struggle was not forgotten.

On 20 August efforts were made by a crowd of men to prevent a farmer from harvesting but the intervention of the Gardai, who arrested one of the men on a charge of intimidation, foiled the attempt. The next day a group of men succeeded in halting operations on a farm, while corn fields on another were found to be spiked with iron bars, ferreting rods, bed parts and rolled barbed wire to hold up harvesting machinery. When these items were removed a similar collection made its appearance on the same fields over the following nights. From then on every field of corn and wheat for reaping was inspected by the owner accompanied by Gardai before harvesting operations commenced (**Irish Press** (IP), 27.8.46; **Irish Times** (IT), 29.8.46).

During the night of Friday, 23 August at Newton, Maynooth 200 tons of hay, haysheds, agricultural implements and a combined harvester were destroyed by fire, with a claim for £2,000 under the malicious injuries acts later being lodged. The farmer concerned was a leading member of the KFA. From then on all cars, cyclists and pedestrians passing through the affected area were searched by the Gardai, while on farms at Castletown, Clane, Collinstown, Pickering Forest, Celbridge and other districts there was a day-and-night Garda patrol (IP, 27.8.46).

James Kavanagh, acting Secretary of the FRW branch, denied emphatically that sabotage had been used by any members of the Federation. Sean Dunne stressed that the FRW had fully instructed all members to act in accordance with law, and that, having made full inquiries, he was satisfied that no members of his union was guilty of sabotage. He complained that police inquiries into the affair were confined to union members but should be widened (**Standard**, 30.8.46).

On Sunday, 25 August farmers from areas not affected arrived in Celbridge and Maynooth to help with the harvest. They brought their own agricultural machinery and in some cases were escorted by Gardai. That night at Blakestown, Leixlip, twenty tons of hay, the property of another leading member of the KFA was destroyed and malice again alleged. The heirs of Captain Moonlight proved impossible to track down, however. On Monday 26th at Clane, an **Irish Press** reporter saw three reapers in one field with 40 helpers in an adjoining hayfield. A photograph on the front page of the same newspaper shows two Gardai in a cornfield walking as escort to the operating harvester (Irish Press, 27.8.46).

By 29 August the town of Celbridge was described in the **Irish Times** as being "in a minor state of siege". Eleven extra Gardai were billeted in the town, while twenty others patrolled outlying districts and were keeping a 'vigilant eye' on the town's 125 strikers. The striking labourers bitterly resented the fact that they were frequently interrogated by the Gardai and claimed harassment at night. One striker declared: "It won't do if your wife or your mother or your sister answers... They have to come up and make sure you're in your own bed." Others commented: "Its worse than the Tan times"; and "Palestine isn't in it" (IT, 29.8.46).

The newspapers reported that sympathy locally was, for the most part, with the strikers. Of the 22 labourers in Celbridge not on strike, it was reported that some had to be escorted to Mass on Sunday by two Gardai, while barmen in some of the town's public houses refused to serve them drink (ibid.).

Because of the attention from the national press towards the end of August, keen interest in the progress of the strike was shown around the country. On 27 August the **Irish Press** reported that branches of the FRW were being organised in Wicklow, Wexford, Cork and Tipperary (IP, 27.8.46). The reference to Cork was substantiated at a special delegate conference of the FRW in October when Sean Dunne said that, while the financial support of the Dublin branch formed the largest single contribution to the strike fund, mention should also be made of their 'Cork comrades' whose aid was available even before the Federation branch was officially formed in that county (MSS, PM, FRW, **Organising Secretary's report to special delegate conference**, October 1946). The national perspective was also presented on 28 August when Sean Dunne was asked in a press interview if the demands for a half-day and a week's holidays would be submitted to farmers in other counties in the near future. He didn't deny that such would be the case (IP, 29.8.46).

On 30 August the Catholic weekly newspaper, the **Standard** launched a very strong attack on the strikers. Though not an official church organ it was, as mentioned above, sold at church gates on Sunday and did have some influence on public opinion. The banner headline on the front page of the **Standard** read *'Farm Strike Threatens Social Order'*. The paper claimed that "a war of sabotage has swept over North Kildare,...where the FRW, a body organised from Dublin, is in conflict with local farmers on issues which seem to us to be more political than social or economic." It went on to say that the 20% of labourers who were on strike should realise that spiking fields and intimidating workers were actions of questionable morality and had been condemned by the "great Popes" (ibid.). While the **Standard** believed that some farmers by their intransigent attitude were damaging the unity of the countryside, the great majority had shown themselves willing to meet the workers so far as their resources would permit.

"The issue of holidays has been met almost entirely by the offer of church holidays, which should always have been free anyway and in most parts of the country still are in consonance with our Catholic and Irish tradition — a tradition which incidentally we do not think the promoters of this strike the best fitted to interpret. Nobody educated in Moscow, or put forward by Moscow educated could be so described" (ibid.).

This latter reference was to the time spent in Moscow by the Larkins. The **Standard**, then warned that efforts were being made "to drive the wedge of class war into other districts of the Irish countryside" also. In the same issue the **Standard's** land correspondent also attacked the strikers and the "urban demogogues" who led them. To choose harvest time to go on strike, he said, was "exactly similar to the refusal of a fire brigade, when called to the scene of a fire, to work its engines unless conditions of service were improved" (ibid.).

At a meeting of the strikers on 1 September at Leixlip, speakers condemned the **Standard** saying it "was not a Catholic paper" and had not been "approved by the Pope" (ibid., 6.9.46). The next issue of the **Standard** carried the front page headline *'Class War Move has Bogged Down in Kildare'* , and went on to claim that its own "exposure" of political rather than social or economic motives "has rattled the Reds element who are endeavouring to foment class war in the countryside" (ibid.). A battle of words then ensued between the **Irish People**, organ of the Irish Labour Party, and the **Standard**. The **Irish People** of 7 September carried the headline, *'Scandalous Attack on Workers of Kildare'*. It referred to the **Standard** as "a self-styled Catholic paper" and accused it of advocating that the men should be deprived of their homes and starved into submission. "Is this a Christian viewpoint?" asked the **Irish People** (Irish People, 7.9.46). The **Standard** retorted that this was a gross calumny, "a piece of disreputable stunt journalism usually adopted by organs anxious to increase a poor circulation" (Standard, 13.9.46).

The **Standard's** 'Land' columnist quoted with approval a Muintir na Tire correspondent who claimed "no normal decent farm worker" would ever want to accept such "a ridiculous and unnatural holiday as a half-day" for himself.

> "In the natural traditional way of farm life — at least since the bad old days have ended — real half-holidays and whole holidays were not those ones which are counted on the clock, but real holidays such as... a wet day on a loft where the conversation was often weird, wonderful and romantic" (ibid., 20.9.46).

The dispute was in essence a clash between the traditional rural outlook which didn't measure by the clock and the modern 'industrial' outlook which had expectations of leisure time. The farm workers during the twentieth century had expectations based on the industrial outlook whereas some employers still held to the traditional relationship.

The struggle continued during the first week of September. Drovers at the Dublin cattle market refused to handle cattle brought to market by farmers from the strike area, with Sean Moore of the Irish Seamen's and Port Workers' Union, to which the drovers belonged, confirming that his union was acting in support of the FRW (IT, 3.8.46). His docker members, following a five-week strike a few weeks previously, had won an additional three days' annual holidays onto the previous week's holidays, so consciousness of the principle involved was high in that particular union.

Some farmers reacted to the blocking of cattle sales by cutting off the milk and vegetable supplies to the homes of strikers, and Sean Dunne alleged that those living in workman's houses owned by farmers were threatened with eviction (IP, 29.8.46). On Sunday, 1 September there was again a big effort by 'flying columns' of farmers from outside the area to save the harvest. An **Irish Press** reporter in the Straffan area saw Gardai and detectives on duty at each field where work was in progress to save over 300 acres of corn which had been left lying because of the lack of labour. In one field between Straffan and Celbridge eleven private cars assembled shortly after lunch. Farmers and their families with pitchforks and rakes proceeded to stack the corn in the field. When the work was completed, they motored, along with the Garda escort, to the next field, and continued in this way till nightfall (ibid., 2.9.46).

In retaliation the FRW declared that the cattle of those farmers from outside who assisted would also be boycotted at the market. This was implemented on 4 September. The newspapers reported that before dawn that day pickets were on patrol on all roads from the county leading to Dublin, while Gardai were on duty to prevent any incidents. Some cattle reached the Dublin market, but 100 pickets, comprising Kildare farm labourers, Dublin cattle drovers and 'others', prevented the livestock from being sold. That night Sean Dunne declared that the strike was by then "very thorough, and a blockade would be imposed on North Kildare" (ibid., 5.9.46).

The situation was then transformed dramatically by the bad weather which created a virtual national emergency. On 4 September the heaviest 24 hours' rainfall since 1938 was recorded at Rathfarnham Castle weather station, which was near Kildare (IT, 5.9.46). That rainfall compounded one of the worst Augusts on record, there being at least some rainfall on every day of the month. The total rainfall for August 1946 was 6.89 inches, the worst since 1924. The abnormal position is illustrated when the previous six years are taken into account. The rainfall in August 1940 was 0.26 inches; 1941 - 2.65; 1942 - 2.59; 1943 - 1.80; 1944 - 2.77; 1945 - 1.16. Throughout the country, the harvest seemed in danger of being lost, while across post-War Europe similar prospects loomed. It was consequently imperative to make the best of every hour of sunshine.

On 5 September the Minister for Agriculture called for volunteers in all areas to help save the harvest. On Sunday, 8 September the Taoiseach, Eamon de Valera, made a special radio broadcast appealing for volunteers from village, town and city to help. The national press took up the appeal and within days there was a tremendous response. Firms in cities and towns closed to allow their workers to go to the country. A Central Harvesting Bureau in Dublin arranged fleets of lorries to ferry volunteers to the country.

The developments put moral pressure on the North Kildare strikers since their blockade was frustrating a drive similar to that initiated in other areas. On 9 September, following a general meeting, the striking labourers submitted proposals to the KFA for a ten-day truce to save the harvest provided that negotiations to end the strike be resumed before the truce expired. The Farmers' Association rejected this offer as totally unacceptable (IP, 10.9.49; 11.9.46). Volunteer labour did however enter the affected area and it was learned in Straffan on 20 September that 50 military personnel, members of the Construction Corps, were helping with the harvest (ibid., 10.9.46). The strikers complained to the Central Harvest Bureau about the volunteer labour and got an assurance on

16 September that none would be sent to the strike area. However, firms continued to send volunteers to the area and on 23 September the FRW decided to picket the premises of any firm that 'refused' cooperation in this matter (ibid., 23.9.46).

On 23 September the new Labour Court established under the Industrial Relations Act 1946 came into operation for the first time. For weeks before, opinion in the Kildare area held that the workers would refer the dispute to the Court once it commenced operations. As with most previous social legislation, agricultural workers were not given the full benefit of the Labour Court. They were excluded from all provisions of the Act, except Part VI, which allowed for the investigation by the Court of strikes in which they were involved. On 25 September, on the advice of their union, the 200 men still on strike decided to refer the dispute to the Labour Court and return to work. The dispute was investigated on 14 November and on 10 July 1947, following which a recommendation was made. There were other significant developments in the intervening period which require examination.

Sean Dunne's contention that the North Kildare strike had been as a "bugle call to the farm workers of every county" was proven correct. When a conference was held a month after the North Kildare strike twelve other counties were represented. By July 1947 a confidential report indicated a membership of about 17,000 in 21 counties. While the total included roadmen and turf workers, the majority were farm labourers.

Table 13. Membership Figures for FRW July 1947

Dublin	3,500	Carlow	300
Kildare	2,102	Monaghan	400
Cork	1,900	Longford	returns awaited
Wexford	1,739	Roscommon	returns awaited
Meath	1,200	Mayo	288
South Tipperary	827	Offaly *	2,000
Mid Tipperary	435	Laois	100
North Tipperary	returns awaited	Sligo	400
Louth	700	Waterford	300 approx
Cavan	650	Donegal	300 approx
Wicklow	552	Clare	300 approx
Westmeath	100		

*(including turf camps)

MSS, PM, FRW, **Confidential Report of General Secretary to Delegates of First Annual Conference, 12.7.47**

By July 1947 the Cork branch contained the third highest number of farm workers. An examination of the origin and growth of the branch in that county illustrates further the difficulties facing those attempting to organise rural labourers. Developments in Cork during the 1940s are also of interest in the light of the detailed study of the county for the years 1919-23 above (Chapters 3 and 4).

At the beginning of the 1946 Cork farm labourers were agitated by the same grievances felt by those in Dublin and Kildare. In April 1946 Con Moynihan of Carrigrohane, four miles west of the city, wrote to Jim Larkin asking that Cork farm workers be accepted into the WUI. Larkin replied that they could not be accepted, but that a new union was being formed and he advised them to contact Sean Dunne (Con Moynihan in interview with D. Bradley, 23.2.82).

In a follow-up letter Sean Dunne explained that the proposed line of advance for the new union, the FRW, represented a departure from usual trade union practice. Having considered the problems encountered by unions catering for rural workers in the past, the Provisional National Executive Committee, FRW, had decided that no attempt should be made by Head Office to form sub-branches in any county until at least a Provisional County (Branch) Committee had been formed. Any departure from that policy, it was felt, would lead to confusion and probably reduce the possibility of achieving cohesive organisation at a later stage (MSS, PM, FRW, **Organising Secretary's Report to Special Delegate Conference**, 26.10.46).

Accordingly, Con Moynihan set about organising county sub-branches. The first one was established in Ballincollig at an open-air meeting, which was held near a wall of the school-ground because the workers didn't have access to a hall. The nucleus of the branch were the seven or eight labourers on both the University College Cork (UCC) farm at Curraheen Road and the Munster Institute, or 'Model Farm', as it was known. Con Moynihan was Secretary, Tim Hallisey, Chairman, and John Sullivan Vice-Chairman (Con Moynihan in interview with D. Bradley, 23.2.82).

They then concentrated on organising the Liberties, those parishes on the perimeter of Cork City. This strategy was similar to that adopted by the Transport Union in 1918 in its push into the Cork countryside. Sub-branches were formed at Douglas, Crosshaven, Togher, Whitescross, Clogheen, Blarney, and Whitechurch. Organisation then spread into East Cork including Carrigtwohill, and north to Fermoy, Glanworth and Kilworth (ibid.).

While organising work was in progress the North Kildare strike occurred. Cork sub-branches collected and contributed significantly to the strike fund, as Sean Dunne openly acknowledged at the end of the strike (MSS, PM, FRW, **Organising Secretary's Report to Special Delegate Conference**, 26.10.46). A Cork County Committee was formed at the beginning of October with Con Moynihan as County Chairman, Dan Desmond, a Labour Party MCC and future TD, as County Secretary, and Tim Hallisey as Vice-Chairman. On 26 October Dan Desmond and Con Moynihan attended the Special Delegate Conference in Dublin (ibid.).

By April 1947 Cork county membership was approaching 1,900 in 37 sub-branches throughout that part of the county east of the Clonakilty-Macroom-Kanturk lines. Discontent was at a high level because there had been no improvement in working conditions since the Kildare strike. From the farmers' viewpoint the most urgent problem was that the continuing bad weather was creating a tillage crisis. On March 18, 1947 the Minister for Agriculture, Patrick Smith, warned that, because of the bad weather of the previous two months, there were still in excess of two million acres to be ploughed if the tillage achievements of the previous year were to be reached (CE, 19.3.47).

A week later Cork Farmers Association (CFA) received a letter from the FRW requesting a conference and setting out the workers' demands as a 12/6 increase on the 44/- and 47/6 rates; a weekly half-day and six days' paid holidays per year (CE, 10.4.47). When CFA had not arranged a conference two weeks later, strike notice was served on 9 April, to take effect a week later (ibid.). The labourers let it be known that they intended to hold up the milk supply to the city during the strike. With memories of the Kildare strike still fresh, a tense situation was created.

Professor Alfred O'Rahilly, President UCC then intervened. He asked the farm workers to suspend strike action while he arranged a conference with the CFA. The strike was postponed but P.D. Lehane, Secretary CFA, informed O'Rahilly that because agricultural wages were under the control of the AWB, which body was reviewing wage levels at that moment, "it would be unwise of us to take any action that may anticipate or embarrass the AWB" (ibid.).

The workers' response was to re-arrange the strike for midnight 23 April. A mass demonstration was arranged for Cork City that evening. Over 1,000 labourers, some of whom had walked ten miles bearing banners with slogans, marched through the city. A public meeting was held at Patrick Street addressed by Sean Dunne, Dan Desmond, Con Moynihan and others. Desmond pointed out that farm workers were paid £2.4s in rural areas, and £2.7.6 in the Milk Board areas near the city. From this 17/6 was deducted if the worker got three meals at his place of employment, a further 2/6 was deducted if he had "a bit of a garden", which left him with "the miserable sum of 25/- or 26/- on which to keep his wife and family" (CE, 24.4.47).

Sean Dunne then announced to the meeting that, following further efforts, Professor O'Rahilly had that very day received a letter from the Chairman of the AWB advising that a meeting of the AWB to fix new minimum rates would be held within weeks. On that basis they would comply with O'Rahilly's appeal to them to again postpone the strike, while reserving the right to strike if the increase proved unacceptable (ibid.). The sceptical among the labourers were pacified by the appearance of the letter from the Chairman, AWB, to Professor O'Rahilly in the **Examiner** the following day (ibid.). The AWB met within a week and granted an increase of 6/- per week throughout the country (ibid., 30.4.47). The Cork branch FRW felt their pressure had played a big part in the quick response of the Board.

Though wage demands had been somewhat satisfied, the AWB had no control over working hours and holidays. The agitation for a half-day and a week's holidays continued in Cork, with the judgement of the Labour Court on the North Kildare dispute being awaited impatiently. At the beginning of June, Sean MacEntee, Minister for Local Government, made an attack on the FRW with innuendos aimed at creating a Red scare. MacEntee declared the FRW agitation was political on behalf of Mr Norton's "International Labour Party". He did not have to emphasise Deputy Larkin's "key position in international politics", nor the significance of the fact that three other members of the Oireachtas were on the committee of the FRW (Brendan Corish, TD, and Senators Thomas Hayden and Michael Smyth). Finally the Minister said all could appreciate "the significance of the association with the union of Mr Sean Dunne, of whom quite a lot might be said" (ibid., 3.6.47).

The Labour Court gave its recommendation on 10 July 1947. While agreeing *in principle* that agricultural workers were entitled, as were industrial workers, to a certain amount of free time and to an annual holiday, it "encountered very great difficulty" in reaching a conclusion on the practical steps to be taken to apply the principle. It pointed out that a farm could not be shut down like a factory or shop; the organisation of the work needed to be adapted to the vagaries of the weather; animals and poultry had to be fed and tended, and cows had to be milked (The Labour Court: **Recommendation on a dispute between FRW and the North Kildare Farmers**, 10.7.47).

While accepting the FRW's point that an agreement encompassing holidays was in operation in County Dublin, the Court said employers had not given any "positive assistance" to the Court on various methods that might be adopted in organising hours of work to arrange holidays.

In conclusion it was decided that:

(i) the Court was not prepared to make a recommendation which, even though expressly limited to the North Kildare area, might be interpreted as applying also to other areas.

(ii) if the working week were shortened by agreement the effect would be that the legal minimum rate of wages would be *reduced*.

(iii) the question of the weekly half-holiday and annual holiday would best be considered in conjunction with the fixing of the legal minimum rates of wages, and that was a matter not for the court, which was restricted to the investigation of disputes, but for the AWB.

(iv) while it supported the principle of a week's holiday and a weekly half-holiday, the Court could not recommend that farmers should be bound to give them in all circumstances (ibid.).

The FRW was totally dissatisfied with this decision and referred to the "effrontery" of the Court in asserting that the working week could not be reduced without a reduction in wages (MSS, PM, FRW, **Early Days of the FRW**). Agitation was stepped up, and in Cork in September a strike was threatened on the issue. The Labour Court refused to investigate on this occasion. Some farmers in County Cork then granted the half-day, which was also gradually extended to farms in Meath, Wicklow and Wexford.

A serious dispute arose in Kilkea, South Kildare when labourers there decided to take the half-day from 14 September, whether the employers approved or not (**Irish People**, 25.10.47). When the harvest was saved ten big employers in the area locked out their 140 men for taking the half-day. The dispute dragged on for over a month, and while the labourers returned to work without getting the half-day, most of the farmers concerned granted it within weeks of resumption (CE, 21.2.48; MSS, PM, FRW, **Early Days of the FRW**).

Similarly, in the Delgany district of County Wicklow, a strike was threatened in January 1948 for the half-day. A compromise was agreed for a half-day nine months of the year, and for an eight hour day from 1 November to 31 January (Irish People, 31.1.48).

The 1948 general election results seemed to augur well for farm workers. Four FRW representatives were elected: Sean Dunne in Co. Dublin, Dan Desmond in South Cork, Brendan Corish in Wexford, and Jim Larkin Jnr. in Dublin South (Central). In addition, with the change of government, the new Tanaiste, William Norton, had championed the farm workers' cause regularly in the past, sponsoring bills for holiday legislation, so that he could be expected to use influence for them now. Within days of the new government being elected, the AWB met and granted a 5/- increase in all areas (CE, 21.2.48), while the government announced that agricultural workers would be given a legal right to paid holidays. The bill for the *Agricultural Workers' Holidays Act, 1950* was duly introduced in 1949.

An additional point of interest with regard to the 1948 election was the manner in which the farmer-labourer question seemed to overshadow the main parties in South Cork. Dan Desmond, who gave his occupation on nominating papers as County Secretary, FRW, headed the poll, while P.D. Lehane of the Cork Farmers' Association was second.

South Cork Constituency		
D. Desmond	Irish Labour Party	7,241
P.D. Lehane	Clann na Talmhan	5,245
S. Buckley	Fianna Fail	5,000
E. O'Neill	Fine Gael	4,488
J. Brown	Fianna Fail	3,502
T. Hales	Clann na Poblachta	2,287
M. O'Driscoll	Fine Gael	1,077

The half-day issue was to create one last controversy. In late 1948, the AWB decided to relate wages to a 50- instead of a 54-hour week from 3 January,

1949. The Minister for Agriculture, James Dillon, was out of the country at the time, but when he returned he disagreed with the AWB decision. In a speech to Offaly County Committee of Agriculture in January 1949, Dillon expressed the hope that the Board would reconsider their "most deplorable" decision soon. This provoked a crisis in the AWB (MSS, PM, FRW, **Early days of the FRW**). The Chairman of the AWB went sick, and the 54-hour week was restored on 4 April. FRW members on state farms refused to revert to the 54 hour week, and the Minister retaliated by cancelling a "plus rate" of 5/-, which had been in operation since September 1948. An FRW news-sheet recalls bitterly, "the farm workers held on to their half-day and Mr. Dillon held on to his five bob until he lost his job as Minister in 1951" (ibid.).

The Minister's intervention is of significance because his predecessors had insisted, since the establishment of the AWB in 1936, that, while they appointed the personnel to it, they had no authority to interfere with the functioning of the board.

A bill, which gave farm workers a weekly half-day with pay, was introduced in the Dail by Sean Dunne on 13.7.1950, and became law on 3.7.51. With the change of government, it was replaced by the *Agricultural Workers' Weekly Half Holidays Act 1952*, which commenced on 23 February, 1953. Farm workers were given two weeks' holidays with pay in 1961 and parity with industrial workers where public holidays were concerned in July 1969.

FEDERATION OF RURAL WORKERS
(CO. CORK)
FARM WORKERS' STRIKE
A MASS DEMONSTRATION

WILL BE HELD

TO-NIGHT (WEDNESDAY)
IN CORK CITY

The Procession will assemble at MARSHS' YARD at 8.15 p.m. Headed by Barrack Street Brass and Reed Band it will march through city to meeting place—PATRICK STREET.
SPEAKERS—Sean Dunne, (General Secretary, F.R.W.), Dan Desmond, M.C.C. (Co. Secretary, F.R.W.) and others.

COME AND HEAR THE FACTS!

From Cork Examiner, 23.4.1947

chapter six

The Agricultural Wages Board 1936–1976

The withdrawal of trade unionism from the farms of all but three counties in the Free State at the end of 1923 heralded the return of laissez-faire to the agricultural sector. The standard of living of farm workers stagnated in the period, 1924–30, along with the economy, and then fell drastically in the wake of the Great Depression. This prompted government intervention in 1936, with the establishment of the AWB. An examination of the 1924–36 period will be followed by an analysis of the AWB's procedures and performance.

(i) From Laissez-faire To Government Intervention, 1924-36

The future policy of the Free State government was clarified in 1924, when the Minister for Agriculture, Patrick Hogan, himself of strong farming stock, accepted the majority report of the Commission on Agriculture, which had been established in 1922. The most significant detail from that report with regard to labourers was that they were not discussed at all. The Minister had *not* included the labourer question in the Commission's terms of reference, which were:
> "to enquire into and report on the causes of the present depression in agriculture, and to recommend such remedies as will secure for Agriculture, and for Industries subsidiary to it, an assured basis for future expansion and prosperity." (Commission on Agriculture, 1924, p.5.)

The six signatories of that Majority report, three farmer representatives and three agricultural 'experts', stressed that the exclusion of the labourer question had hampered their work severely.
> "We have, moreover, been restricted in our discussion by the omission from the terms of reference of the question of relations between employers and employed, without a consideration of which it is extremely difficult to reach any satisfactory conclusion on many of the problems which it was our duty to examine" (ibid., p.70).

Even if there was a hint there to the Minister that the labourer question needed to be examined, it was ignored, and the possibility of reintroducing the Agricultural Wages Board was never entertained during the next nine years of Cumann na nGaedheal administration. That Government acted on the belief that economic policy should be "directed to maximise the farmer's income, because, the farmers being the most important section of the population, everything that raised their income raised the national income of the country" (An obituary article on Patrick Hogan by G. O'Brien, *Studies*, xxv, Sept 1936, p.353-68). Ireland, this Government believed, could not follow the example of certain other countries, differently situated, where the provision of food for the urban population, or the solution of the unemployment problem, governed the aims of agriculture.

Thus, the labourer's wages, being a cost of production, must not be encouraged to exceed a level that would interfere with the farmer's prosperity. When the farmer's wealth had been increased, labourers' prosperity would be "incidentally secured". Furthermore, the Government, as recommended by the Majority Report, was in favour of the type of agriculture in which Ireland had shown itself to have the greatest comparative advantage during 80 years, namely the raising of dry cattle, which many claimed would require less labour than tillage (though the signatories of the Majority report denied this).

The Majority report was also opposed to the granting of direct assistance by tariffs, subsidies, or guaranteed prices, and since the guarantee of a minimum wage had, in the past, been linked with the price guarantees for grain to the farmer, the discouragement of this latter was unlikely to enhance prospects of intervention on wages.

Finally, any hopes of acquiring land, as a substitute for wages agitation, that labourers might have nursed through the War and revolutionary years, received a setback with the Majority report pointing out that no scheme of re-distribution, no matter how drastic, could ever effect more than a partial solution, as there was insufficient land to give every *existing occupier* an economic holding — with not even a mention of the landless labourer. That report further recommended that the "settlers must be drawn from men and families in whom the habits of industry and hard work attaching to tillage farming have been strongly implanted" (p.70). The under-employed or unemployed labourer of the cattle-raising East, or dairying South, was the most unlikely candidate to fit that role. Then the signatories, whose views the Minister accepted, stressed that they would "strongly deprecate the allotment of land to persons merely because they are contiguous to the land to be divided" (ibid., p.35). No one lived nearer to such land than the labourer whose cottage was on it, but now the one point on which he might have an advantage was being played down in importance.

That there was an alternative to the policy accepted by the Minister for Agriculture is indicated by the fact that the Minority Report submitted by Thomas Johnson and Michael Duffy, the Irish Labour Party and Trade Union Congress representatives on the Commission, was in sharp contrast with the other.

The signatories of that report stated:

"We are emphatically of opinion that State policy respecting agriculture must be guided by a clear recognition of the principle that in the utilization of the national resources, including the land, individual self-interest must be subordinated to the national welfare."

And that the purpose of agriculture should be directed:
"Firstly, to satisfy the needs of the people of this country and, secondly, to supply the demand from other countries for commodities of a quality or kind which we can promote to advantage" (p.79).

The authors were convinced that the prosperity of agricultural Ireland would depend largely upon the use of tillage crops for feeding livestock of all kinds, and the production and sale of animal foods of high quality, particularly milk, cream, butter, bacon and eggs. Furthermore, the Government should guarantee a minimum price for limited quantities of wheat in order to encourage its revival.

With respect to the labourer, such a policy would ensure employment, in support of which opinion the signatories quote J.R. Campbell of the Department of Agriculture, a witness to the Commission, as saying that even one third of a farm tilled would employ five to six times more labour (p.77). Then, too, the precedent of the new state's intervention in agriculture would create a favourable environment and provide the statistical data to which labourers' claims for external adjustment of the wage mechanism could be related more readily.

The need for an awareness of such statistical data was clearly demonstrated during the twenties and early thirties, when there were constant changes in agricultural prices, consumer price indices and wage levels. Those changes led to allegations of exploitation of workers by employing farmers, and counter-claims of inability to pay.

Being determined solely by supply and demand in the context of deepening depression, money wages fell steadily 1924-32, and then drastically 1933-36. Real wages, however, the purchasing power of the labourer's income — meagre though it was — held at slightly above the 1924 level until 1933, because the cost of living index fell slightly more than wages during those years. Contemporaries on all sides were sceptical about the value of the cost of living index, and it was particularly limited with respect to farm labourers since the index was based on the average purchases by wage earners in towns, whose household requirements would have been different to those of the rural labourers, as Mr. Lemass indicated in the Dail in 1936 (see, for example, Dail Reports, Vol 64, col 644, 19.11.36). Nevertheless, it does provide concrete evidence of conditions. In 1934 (Table 14) the cost of living began to *rise* relative to the previous years, while wages dropped another 5%, the biggest decrease since 1923. The 1/3 lost on the average wage in 1934 imposed very severe restrictions on what was already a subsistence standard of living, while in 1935 the labourer's position deteriorated further.

The response to accusations that labourers were being exploited during the post-1924 period was to point to the catastrophic fall in wholesale agricultural prices. The agricultural price index had risen from 100 in 1911-13 to 288 in 1920, but by 1924 it had fallen to 160, and had slumped to 83 by 1935. Then farmers who had borrowed heavily from the banks during wartime prosperity had great difficulties in repaying. Furthermore, the rains of 1924 led to widespread livestock disease, causing distress which in the western counties was described as the worst since the famine of 1879. Table 14 shows that the percentage drop in agricultural prices was every year far greater than that in wages. Thus, in 1926, when wages fell by 2.8%, agricultural prices fell by 12.4%, in 1930 the corresponding figures were 6.7% and 22%, while in 1935 they were 19% and 48.1% respectively.

Table 14. Percentage Change In 3 Factors Related In Determining Relative Positions Of Labourers' Wages And Employing Farmers' Incomes, 1924-35

Year	Cost Of Living Index Mid-July	Agricultural Wages Index Mid-July	Agricultural Prices Index
1924	183	100 (26/3)	160
1925	+ 2.7%	100	- 1.4%
1926	- .55%	- 2.8%	- 12.4%
1927	- 6.6%	- 2.8%	- 17.6%
1928	- 5.5%	- 5.9%	- 14.3%
1929	- 4.9%	- 4.8%	- 12.9%
1930	- 8.2%	- 6.7%	- 22.0%
1931	- 14.2%*	- 7.6%	-
1932	- 16.4%	- 10.5%	- 38.8%
1933	- 18.6%	- 15.2%	- 47.5%
1934	- 16.9%	- 20.0%	- 47.5%
1935	- 14.8%	- 19.0%	- 48.1%

* Change from mid-July to mid-August henceforth

Cost of living index in **Irish Trade Journal** (ITJ), August 1930, p.151 and December 1936, p.213;
Wages index in ITJ, May 1930, p.116 and ITJ 1936;
Agricultural Prices in ITJ, February 1931, p.85 and ITJ, 1936

The ultimate consequence of this development, however, was that while employing farmers sympathised annually with the low standard of living of the labourers, they pointed out that their own incomes did not allow them to pay higher wages.

Close examination of the distribution of agricultural wealth produced in 1924-35, however, suggests that the depression created a smokescreen, whereby some of the big farmers, with whom 75% of the labourers worked, attempted to get back from their workers some of the profits they lost due to the fall in income. The calculations used here were frowned upon as having a pseudo-scientific basis when first put forward by Dr. Ryan, Minister for Agriculture, in 1936 (Dail Debates, Vol 64, col 210-5, 11.11.36). The generalised nature of the figures leads the contemporary analyst to be suspicious of them too, but they do provide a yardstick for comparing the relative positions of big farmers and labourers.

Total remuneration to agriculture in 1926-7 was £59,250,000. From statistics at the time, it was calculated that paid agricultural workers got, on average, £66 each, which meant that farmers and relatives in 1926-7, if the remainder was divided between them, got an average £93 (ibid., col 211). In 1934-5, agricultural output got a return of £40,500,000. Deducting the costs of rents, rates, tradesmen's bills, etc., and estimating the total labourer bill on the average rate of £54.12s per annum for 127,000 workers, we are left with £27,620,000 to share between farmers and relatives. The Minister for Agriculture estimated an average income of £51 per farmer and relative in 1936 (ibid., col 214), because he did not then have the 1936 Census figures, which showed a reduction of 28,000. Thus, the average rate for farmers and relatives would have been £55 per annum in 1934-5, similar to that for a labourer.

The obvious point, of course, is that this income was not distributed equally among the farming families. More than half of the agricultural population lived on holdings of under £10 valuation, while, in 1934, 22,750 farmers and relatives were in receipt of unemployment benefit. Therefore, the small farmers were receiving a smaller share of total agricultural income than £55, which implied that the share of the strong farmers was well above £55 per year.

Only 32,000 labourers worked on farms under 50 acres, so that the big farmers, who employed three-quarters of the wage earners, were still, in 1934, despite the depression and economic war, in receipt of incomes well over £55 per annum. They did not share that income with their men. A survey was undertaken in 1935 to discover what were the average wages paid on the different size farms (ibid., col 207). The counties involved comprised Meath, Wexford, Cork, Tipperary and Galway. On farms under 50 acres, it was discovered, 22/- was the average wage in 1935. On farms of 50-100 acres, it was only 20/-. These findings are in line with the assertion of Mr. Pattison, TD, in the Dail in November 1936 when he declared:

> "As a member of the Court of Referees for many years, my experience has been that in all cases the poor working farmers treat their men generously. It is the big farmer, who can go to the races, and who can drive around in his motor car, who does not provide the men who live in with sleeping accommodation under the same roof as himself. They are forced to sleep in some back shed" (ibid., col 307).

If the average rate of wages seemed miserable, the real problem was that in places labourers worked for far less than the average.

From Table 15 it can be seen that, by 1935, 9.8% in County Cork and 13.2% of labourers in the Saorstat received a wage on which it would have been very difficult to live when the movement of the cost of living index in Table 14 is taken into account. Allegations that rates even far lower than 17/- were being paid were substantiated. Indeed, Mr. Finlay, TD, who employed "a good many hands", admitted in the Dail that he was one of them, on the grounds that he could not pay more.

Table 15. Variations In The Wage Rates For Farm Labourers In 1931 And 1935			
	Saorstat Eireann	*County*	*Cork*
	1935	*1931*	*1935*
Under 17/-	13.2%	3.2%	9.8%
17/- to 20/-	15.9%	5.6%	16.9%
20/- to 25/-	46.4%	40.6%	41.1%
25/- to 30/-	15.0%	32.0%	18.2%
30/- to 35/-	7.0%	14.0%	9.1%
Over 35/-	2.5%	4.6%	4.9%

Dail Reports, Volume 64, columns 205-6, 11.1.1936

"When others like myself pay a man 10/- or 12/- on a Saturday night and when he takes that home to his wife and family, I am wondering how he is going to maintain them after paying for his cottage" (ibid., col 261).

But then he observes:

"It is only natural if you have a loaf and if you are going to divide it with another that you will be tempted to keep the big end yourself" (ibid., col 263).

The evidence of other TDs also indicated the low wages that some labourers received. William Norton put himself on record in the House as saying that hundreds of labourers in Kildare were working for as low as 12/6 (ibid., col 294). T.J. Murphy asserted that the men who "had the courage to refuse 2/-, 3/-, 4/- and 5/- per week" were deprived of unemployment assistance. Murphy then gave evidence of the most appalling conditions of all when he told how, at sittings of the Court of Referees, he had come across cases of young men being hired out from industrial schools, and given no pay other than their food (ibid., col 305-6). Unorganised, the farm labourer found himself at the bottom of the pile in a society dominated by depression and economic stagnation.

Pressures weighed on him so much that he was unable or unwilling to fight for change. Unemployment and under-employment dominated rural life. At the same time small farmers and their relatives assisting were being forced to emigrate or migrate, so that any potential for class consciousness on the labourers' side was blunted by seeing landowners, though not their *own* employers, in severe difficulties. In 1930, there were 22,176 people on the live register of unemployed. The Unemployment Assistance Act of 1933 extended help to persons who had never been employed or gainfully occupied, as well as to many who were working on their own accord, but whose means did not exceed a statutory limit. Thus, there were 22,750 farmers and their relatives in receipt of benefit in 1935, giving an indication of the conditions under which such people lived prior to the implementation of the 1933 Act.

From the farm labourer's viewpoint, those small farmers in receipt of benefit would have been competitors for labouring work during the 20s, and still were after 1933 at those times of the year between March and October when assistance was restricted.

Table 16 indicates the extent to which under-employment added further to the labourers' insecurity, making those in 'full-time' jobs more reluctant to complain about wages and conditions.

The number of permanent workers remained in the upper eighty thousand region throughout the period, but the number of those taken on temporarily rose steadily from 45,755 in 1927 to 61,690 in 1931, and was still 60,782 in 1936. Comparison of these figures with the Census figures for 1926 and 1936 indicates just how many of those 'temporarily employed' were out of work at Census time. In 1926, the Census recorded 125,972 labourers, but on 1 June, 1927 there were 133,199. The 1936 figures are even more emphatic, with the Census listing 127,834 and the **Statistical Abstracts** showing 150,752 labourers on 1 June.

Table 16. Number Of Males (Non-Family) Employed On Farms, 1927-36, Inclusive Of Those Under 18 Years Of Age

Year	Permanent Workers	Temporarily Employed
1927	87,444	45,755
1928	89,371	47,640
1929	88,805	59,315
1930	88,782	58,391
1931	89,594	61,690
1932	88,619	60,320
1933	88,819	58,978
1934	90,032	63,545
1935	88,977	64,186
1936	89,970	60,782

Statistical Abstract, 1930, Table 45, page 35; 1934, Table 55, page 41; 1936, Table 53, page 50

Emigration had its psychological effects also. It was farmers and relatives assisting who emigrated during the 1926-36 period, their numbers falling by 28,109 from 531,418 to 503,309 (**Census of Population**, 1951, Vol 5, Appendix p.154). While the number of permanent labourers actually increased during the period, the fact that others in the agricultural sector were obliged to leave could not but have a negative influence on the aspirations of the labourer.

During the early thirties, as in the twenties, the ITGWU regretted that it could not accept labourers into the union as their low income would not enable them to maintain continuous membership. Nevertheless, that union maintained an interest in the plight of those labourers and the **1932 Annual Report** informs us that after an "earnest consideration of the problem the Union had come to the conclusion that there was urgent need for an AWB and fixing of minimum wages" (p.9). The Union Executive then took the matter up with the Trades Union Congress (ITUC), succeeded in getting their viewpoint adopted, which in turn led to a practical scheme for Wages Boards being pressed on the Minister by the Labour Party.

In his General President's address at the Annual Conference of the ITGWU in May 1936, Foran declared that after several years' agitation they had received an undertaking that the Dail would legislate in favour of Wages Boards (ibid., 1935). The introduction of the Bill aroused very strong opposition, nonetheless, and was the occasion of much political manoeuvring. When asked in the Dail on 31 October, 1935 if he proposed to introduce Wages Boards, in view of the fact, as Deputy Davin alleged, that in some areas agricultural workers were in receipt of wages which were actually lower than the amount of unemployment assistance to which they would be entitled, the Minister for Agriculture replied that no such proposals were "in contemplation". However, when pressed by William Norton the Minister gave the politically adept answer that the proposal was not in contemplation but neither had they considered abandoning it (Dail Reports, Vol 59, col 235, 31.10.35).

Farmer opposition to Wages Boards in 1935-36 was based on several arguments. The first was the by now familiar contention that prosperity in agriculture must precede wage guarantees. The **Farmers' Gazette** reflected another point on which farmer opposition was based: "The real trouble, that Mr. Norton [leader of the Labour Party in the Dail] avoids or would evade is the relative affluence of the railway porters and the urban industrial and factory workers" (Farmers Gazette, 18.4.36). This point of view stressed that farm workers were taking their expectations from living standards in the towns rather than the countryside.

Opposition to the proposed Bill also came from the Department of Finance. A memorandum on the proposed Bill was circulated to members of the Executive Council on 7 March, 1936 by the Department of Agriculture. On 21 March the Department of Finance, on behalf of its Minister, responded with a memo to the cabinet. It began by criticising the proposed legislation on the grounds that there had been insufficient preliminary inquiries as to the best mode of operation for the Wages Board. The Department then went on to express an attitude which echoed that of the employing farmers:

> "It may be a fact that in this country agricultural labourers in places are paid relatively low wages and it is probably true that they would have the sympathy of every section of the community for any reasonable effort to improve their conditions. The really important matter, however, is the ability of the farmers to pay and the consumers to bear the cost of better wages than they are doing and the case for an elaborate system of a Central Wages Board and Regional Wages Committees stands or falls on that. The Department of Agriculture have made no effort whatever to elucidate that supremely important aspect of the problem" (State Paper Office, S8744, **Department of Finance Memorandum to the Executive Council,** 21.3.1936, p.3).

The implication is that if the farmers seemed unable to pay, then it was necessary for the labourer to suffer on, having as sustenance the sympathy of every section of the community. Despite the fact that they were so rigorous in criticism of the Department of Agriculture, the authors of the memo made no effort to define what they would consider "any reasonable effort" to improve labourer conditions. The sources for determining the farmers' ability to pay used in this study, above, were readily available for the Department's financial experts.

The Finance memorandum states several other arguments to strengthen its case against Wages Boards. They would have "immediate and serious reactions" on Government expenditure in relation to Public Health Works, afforestation, arterial drainage, Land Commission improvement schemes, relief schemes, agricultural colleges and preparatory colleges. As well as tending to drive farmers out of production, the Boards would lead to "disemployment in the present and unemployment in the future of agricultural labour" (ibid., p.5). Furthermore, they would also lead to "agitation for increases in wages in every form of industrial employment", possibly leading to strikes and labour unrest in urban areas. Because they would make agricultural exports less competitive by pushing up the cost of production, the Boards would be the cause of weakening the country's currency, "and devaluation will become an increasing menace to owners of mobile capital, who will seek to safeguard their possessions against that danger by transferring them abroad" (ibid., p.6).

The Department of Finance also saw political reasons for opposing the Bill. It will have the effect of "handing over the agricultural industry to the Trade Unions". Then, suggesting that Labour Party pressure might be the motive for the proposed introduction of the Boards, the memo declared:

"The Labour Party, which is not likely to be faced in the near future with the task of taking office and assuming responsibility, is very free with suggestions of this kind, and the irresponsible manner in which they are made, and the large number of them, would appear to render it all the more advisable to offer resistance now" (ibid., p.7).

Concern for Dr. Ryan's ability to handle Labour Party pressure, however, was shown to be unwarranted. When it came to introducing the Bill, the Minister extracted the maximum political advantage. Dr. Ryan moved leave to introduce the Bill on 12 August, which conveniently happened to be the day before the Dail adjourned for the summer recess. This prompted 'D.S.' of **The Irish Independent** to comment that when the Bill was introduced, "not only were many Deputies absent in body, but many more were absent in spirit" (13.8.1936). The introduction of the Bill also happened to be a short time before two important by-elections, in Galway and in Wexford, where there was a heavy concentration of agricultural labourers. All political parties were capable of anticipating the response of those workers to news of the introduction of wages legislation. Therefore, James Dillon objected to granting leave to introduce the Bill for the purpose of eliciting information on it, leading to bantering from all sides in the Dail.

Dillon's argument boiled down to what employing farmers had been saying for the previous fifteen years about inability to pay, and the point which had been the basis of Cumann na nGaedheal (now Fine Gael) policy during the same period — that economic prosperity would have to precede any wage legislation. The Government, said Dillon, was attempting to achieve "that classical impossibility, the squeezing of blood from a turnip or water from a stone" (Dail Reports, Vol 63, col 2573, 12.8.1936).

The second stage of the Bill on 11 November occupied five and a half hours of business time and afforded Dillon the full opportunity to display his eloquence. Every aspect of the labourers' wages question was touched on during the debate. Other Fine Gael deputies echoed Dillon's objections to the Boards, but they did not in the end vote against the Bill, which had passed through the Dail by the end of November 1936. It remained to be seen to what extent the hopes and fears expressed for the Wages Board would be realized.

(ii) The Procedures Of The Agricultural Wages Board, 1936-1976

The establishment of a Wages Board was a belated recognition by the government that laissez-faire had failed in the sphere of farmer-worker bargaining. It would now require strenuous efforts by the government on behalf of the employees to redress the situation. Such efforts were not forthcoming. In fact, the government, during the 1940s in particular, had a vested interest in keeping farm wages at a low level.

Other factors which retarded the work of the Board were its own cumbersome procedural machinery, the absence from its constitution of definite guidelines in relation to aspects of policy making, and the continued exclusion from its jurisdiction, during its forty-year history, of the question of working conditions, as distinct from the determination of wage levels.

On the other hand, it needs to be stressed that the AWB did make some positive contributions. The establishment of the *principle* of regulation of relationships on the farm was in itself a step forward.

Table 17 indicates the results of the Board's intervention over seven of its first nine years of operation.

The principal functions of inspectors were to investigate complaints regarding the payment of wages at less than the minimum rates prescribed, to adjust disputes between employers and employees, to carry out miscellaneous inspection work, and to inquire into applications for permits of exemption from the provisions of the Act for people who were incapacitated and thus unable to perform sufficient work to merit the minimum wage. Table 17 indicates that most arrears were paid without the requirement of legal proceedings. Thus, the knowledge that an inspector of the Board might call, or that a complaint might be lodged, with the posibility of subsequent prosecution, stimulated

Table 17. Results Of Intervention By AWB, 1937–1945

Year	No. of Inspectors	Complaints	Arrears Recovered	Legal Proceedings	Visits	Interviews With Employers	Interviews With Employees
1937-8	8	1,500	N.A.	8	12,000	—	—
1940	8	622	N.A.	18	14,255	12,531	17,929
1942	2 (6 on emergency war duty)	902	£4,472	6	2,417	1,662	3,088
1943	2	830	£6,012	4	2,605	1,791	3,379
1944	3	1,145	£5,629	4	2,822	2,244	3,938
1945	3	1,066	£4,311	1	2,646	2,059	3,699

State Paper Office, S8744, File 13503A, S11689, Reports Of Proceedings Of A.W.B., 1937-1945 irresponsible employers, at least to some degree, to improve the position.

In both the Irish and international contexts for wage-fixing machinery, the Wage Board as constituted in 1936 had many familiar aspects. It was closely modelled on the Board that had been established under the provisions of the *Corn Production Act*, 1917 and which had operated in Ireland until 1921 (see Chapter 2). Great Britain, in comparison, was in 1936 operating under the 1924 Act, which had in fact merely re-introduced the provisions of the *Corn Production Act*. It was only with the passing of the Agricultural Wages Act, 1947, that the British system was reformed. Farm workers in France, Denmark, the Netherlands and Czechoslovakia had all been placed in a position to make collective bargains before 1936. Scotland and Northern Ireland, however, had no agricultural wage-fixing machinery until 1939.

The AWB of 1917 was constituted on very similar lines to Trade Boards in industry. From their origin in the state of Victoria, Australia, under the *Factories and Shops Act*, 1896, Trade Boards had come to play a significant role in the United Kingdom by 1920. There were fifty seven of them in the UK at the end of 1920, of which fifteen were in Ireland, including six in clothing related industries. The Saorstat, in its early years, was unproductive of social legislation in this area, but the Fianna Fail government had taken the initiative with the introduction of Trade Boards for packing in 1934 and for the handkerchief and household piece goods industry in 1935.

With regard to the vital question of representativeness, Trade Boards were invariably composed of an equal number from the employer and employee sides, together with one or more independent persons. The representatives of employers and workers, numbering anywhere from two to ten, were nominated by their respective organisations. In the absence of organisation, they were appointed by the appropriate state authority, which also appointed independent members.

In 1934 Professor B.F. Shields commented that:

"The success of the trade board system has been largely due to the fact that the representative members can bring to bear on the discussions a good, practical knowledge of the technique and conditions of the trade on which they can speak freely; while the disinterested members, representing the public, can act as conciliators in reconciling differences and can express their considered opinion, after listening to the arguments, on the various proposals submitted for consideration, and can exercise their vote on behalf of rival propositions" (**The Minimum Wage**, *JSSISI, xxxxvii*, 1933-4).

Unfortunately, as far as the AWB of 1936 was concerned, the Professor's views seemed idealistic. From the beginning there was bitter controversy on the very question of the AWB's "representativeness". With regard to distribution of numbers the Board measured up without difficulty. It comprised four employer, four worker and three 'neutral' members, to quote the official terminology, plus a neutral chairman. However, it was with regard to the *method* of appointing members that the lasting criticism arose. In 1917, as seen above (Chapter 2), those nominated to speak for farm workers were drawn from their own organisations. Munster counties were represented by the Land and Labour Association, the South-East by the Irish Trade and Labour League, and Dublin and adjoining counties by the ITGWU. Since the first two organisations did not exist in 1936, and the ITGWU had ceased to cater for farm workers by then, the Minister for Agriculture was obliged to exercise other criteria in selecting members. His political opponents claimed that the chief criterion used in selection was allegiance to Fianna Fail.

Certainly, the fact that the chairman of the Board for its first nineteen years, William O'Leary, was an ex-Fianna Fail TD, provided ammunition for such attacks. Thus, William Norton, leader of the Labour Party, in 1937 claimed that the chairman was the nominee of the Minister, was paid by the Minister (£750 a year) and controlled by the Minister. "As he was subject to the control of the Minister, it could be taken that he had in mind largely what the desires of the Minister were when he fixed 24/- a week" (The Labour Party, **Annual Report**, 1937, p.160).

The Labour Party and ITUC, which had been pressing for an AWB since 1932, resented the fact that they were not consulted on the appointment of worker members.

In addition to the twelve-member central board, the AWB also comprised five area committees, each covering five or six neighbouring counties, and on which there was an equal number of worker and employer members, ranging from five to eight. The Chairman of the Central Board also presided at the meetings of the Area Committee, held twice yearly on average.

In this context, the relevant point concerning the Area Committees was the allegation that they were much more prone to manipulation than the Central Board. This was because they were re-nominated on a yearly basis, whereas the Central Board was re-appointed every three years. Thus Jeremiah Hurley, the Labour TD for East Cork, complained in 1937 that two Cork members who had become "somewhat troublesome to the Board" were dropped after the first year to be replaced by two "yes-men" of the Fianna Fail party (ibid., p.161). Michael Ronayne of Ballincollig demanded to know in 1937 what branch of labour "would like to have its representatives in wage negotiations picked for it by employers or by the Government?... That was the position of the agricultural worker today... Farmers' representatives were mainly of the type which lived near the city, and were known as 'gentlemen farmers', but in his opinion, they were neither gentlemen nor farmers" (ibid., p.162).

Ronayne's last quoted sentence contains the admission that the representation of farmers on the Wages Board was also less than satisfactory. Over the next twenty years we find labourers' spokesmen calling for farmers' organisations to be given the right to choose the members for that sector of the Board. Thus, J. Tully TD moved a motion at the ITUC 60th Conference in July 1954 calling for the Agricultural Wages Acts to be amended to (1) give trade unions catering for agricultural workers the right to nominate the workers' representatives on the AWB, and (2) to give the Farmers' Associations the right to nominate the employers' representatives (ITUC **Annual Report**, 1954, p.170).

Concern for the interests of the employers was hardly what motivated Mr. Tully and his supporters. Rather it was the realization that more effective pressure could be put on farmers' organisations to implement collective agreements than might be applied to farmers on an individual basis.

When the Federation of Rural Workers was founded in 1946, one of its demands was the right to nominate the workers' members to the AWB. That union made significant advances during the three years that followed (Chapter 5) and, while its claim to nominate members was never recognised officially, Ministers for Agriculture from 1950 onward appointed the same three Federation leaders to the board continuously for fifteen years, two of them, indeed, up until the Board was abolished in 1976. That concession was not sufficient to halt the union's agitation on the *principle* of the right to nominate members.

Representation on the Area Committees continued to be less satisfactory. During the 1950s labourer leaders continued to express discontent with what appeared to them to be the inefficient and biased method of appointing the employee representatives. Tully documented one of the most bizarre cases of all when he announced that "in one case, the workers' representative was a builder's labourer in Birmingham" (ibid., p.171). Ironically enough, the leader of Mr. Tully's own party, William Norton, was Tanaiste and Minister for Industry and Commerce at the time of that allegation in 1954. Norton agreed that the AWB "is balanced against the workers... and this government will introduce an agricultural Labour court with better representation for agricultural workers" (ibid., p.155). That promise, however, was not fulfilled.

*

Several aspects of the Board's method of procedure and power structure also caused dissatisfaction among worker representatives. An element of mystery surrounded its activities, because members were sworn to secrecy as to the business transacted at its meetings. Furthermore, it was not until 1961 that the Chairman allowed copies of the minutes to be circulated to members. From 1961 onwards, some members of the Board resorted to the tactic of leaking information on meetings to the press in order to gain sympathy for their side. That was the case following the 114th Meeting of the Board on 9 August, 1961, when progress was so unsatisfactory to worker members that the FRW decided to call for strike action. The next day's newspapers carried headlines that competed with the **Dublin Evening Mail**'s one — *"90,000 Farm Hands Serve Strike Notice"* (Dublin Evening Mail, 10.8.61; **Irish Independent**, 10.8.61). Strike action, however, was averted.

The 1936 Act, in theory, gave exceptional powers to the Chairman of the AWB. In the context of so much secrecy and rumour that surrounded the activities of the Board in the following years, it is not surprising that many were convinced that he acted in a dictatorial fashion. In actual fact, apart from the earliest years of the Board's operation, the Chairman did not use his power of voting at all. But many were more impressed by the fact that the Act stated: "The Chairman of the Board shall constitute a quorum" (*Agricultural Wages Act, 1936*, Section 12 (3)), so that theoretically the Chairman could decide matters without reference to other members.

Of more immediate relevance, however, was that section of the Act allowing the Chairman to fix the rate himself, unless there was agreement among the worker and employer representatives (which was rare). In this context, the first order of the Board was unfortunate. A blanket rate of 24/- per week was fixed for the whole country. However, in the Dublin Area Committee, worker members had demanded 40/- per week, and employer representatives were agreeable to fixing the rate at 31/6. To have 24/- imposed in that context seemed dictatorial and grossly unfair to workers' spokesmen. The problem was rectified in 1938, when a separate rate of 33/- was settled for the greater part of Co. Dublin.

The nature of the statutory relationship between Area Committees and the Board resulted in procedure being cumbersome and slow-moving. The Board, in the final analysis, held total power for the fixing of rates, but it had a statutory obligation to consult the Area Committees, and to take their "recommendations" into account when determining a rate. Since the Area Committees were made up of an equal number of farmers and workers, plus the Chairman, who was excluded from voting, in practice the two sides rarely agreed on a rate. Voting on proposals was normally deadlocked, with the consequence that two conflicting recommendations were forwarded to the Board.

The statutory procedure took three months, which was another source of grievance. It was required that the Board meet first of all and pass a motion (and that was an issue in itself) giving notice to the Area Committees of its intention to fix new minimum rates of wages. The Committees were then obliged to meet and submit their proposals within a period of two months. Finally, the Board met once more to consider the Committees' recommendations, when a new rate might, or might not, be agreed.

Since the role of the Area Committees was limited, that of bona fide farmer and worker representatives predictable, and given that the Chairman did not exercise his right to vote for most of the forty-year existence of the Board, it follows that the three independent members of the Board had a crucial role to play. The criteria by which they were guided were thus of the utmost importance. The Agricultural Wages Act, 1936, gave them no guidance on factors to be considered, merely requiring the Board to "from time to time, as they think proper, by order fix for each wages district the minimum rates of wages for agricultural workers for time work." (*Agricultural Wages Act, 1936*, Introduction.)

An investigation of the legislation for, and operations of, other minimum wage fixing bodies in various countries prior to 1936 reveals that a number of distinct principles had been evolved for the settlement of a wages question by such bodies (see Shields, p.73). Pope Pius XI, in his Encyclical **Quadragessimo Anno**, considered a living wage, the capacity of the business to pay, along with "the economic welfare of the people of a country" to be crucial determinants. That coincided with the guiding factors in several European countries.

An examination of British Trade Boards in 1922 showed that they had evolved seven criteria. Under the Acts of 1909 and 1918, British Trade Boards were not given guidelines for their purpose, but an expert witness, in evidence before the Cave Committee on Trade Boards in Great Britain in 1922, stated that they were governed by seven factors: the cost of living index number; the nature of the work; the degree of skill and experience required for its adequate performance; the character and economic position of the industry concerned; the wages paid to other comparable trades; the relation in which the class of workers concerned stood to other workers; and the capacity of the industry to pay (ibid.).

With regard to the Irish AWB in 1936, this question of criteria was to be of more fundamental importance even than it had been for any earlier AWB in the British Isles, because, of the total of the six AWBs established in the British Isles during the thirty-year period 1917–1947, only the Irish Board of 1936 was **not** required to have regard to prescribed guidelines. The Agricultural Wages Board for Ireland 1917-21, along with its counterparts in Scotland, and that in England and Wales, was governed by the "limitation" clause in the Corn Production Act, 1917, which stated:

> "5. (6) In fixing minimum rates... the A.W.B. shall, so far as is practicable, secure for able-bodied men wages which, in the opinion of the Board, are adequate to promote efficiency and to enable a man in an ordinary case to maintain himself and his family in accordance with such standard of comfort as may be reasonable in relation to the nature of his occupation." (**Memorandum** submitted to AWB, 13.12.62, by Patrick Murphy, Vice-President, FRW, p.18; copy in possession of members of the Board.)

The Northern Ireland AWB, set up in 1939, was governed by the above limitation clause, with the additional measure that "the Board shall have regard to the economic position of agriculture in the area to which the minimum rate is to be applied" (ibid.).

Thus, after 1936, the independent members of the Irish AWB, not being governed by such limitations, were obliged to decide on their own criteria. An examination of their voting record over the forty years of the Board's existence reveals that their decisions were inconsistent. On occasions, they were governed solely by the recommendations of the Area Committees. At other times, it was the direct or indirect demands of government policy that ruled. Nor can such inconsistency be explained by changes in 'neutral' personnel on the Board. One neutral member, an academic from Dublin University, served for the entire forty years of the Board's operation, while others tended to be removed by death rather than by incurring the displeasure of the Minister for Agriculture.

In the course of taking oral evidence during 1942, the Commission on Vocational Organisation endeavoured to ascertain the principles that influenced the Board in fixing rates. "It appeared that the Board made its determinations not on any definite principles or as the result of detailed enquiry into prices and production costs, but by averaging the recommendations of the regional committees." (Commission's Report, p.136). That reply was less than satisfactory, however, as an examination of the Board's performance over the years will reveal.

(iii) The Performance Of The Agricultural Wages Board, 1936-76

The average earnings of a farm worker during the year 1936 was 22/-, and his standard of living was admitted on all sides to be at subsistence level. Thus, when the AWB set a rate of 24/- in 1937, it was not bringing about a signficant change in that standard. It was pointed out at the time, that the cost of food alone, on the Board's own calculation, showed how low 24/- per week was. The Board was required to determine the price to be charged for meals which the labourer took at the farmer's house. Obviously, those labourers living-in took all such meals, but it was not uncommon for the married labourer to take some, at least, of his meals at the farmhouse also. The relevance of the Board's calculations on food, therefore, was wide ranging.

Breakfast cost the worker 6 1/2d per day, dinner 10d, evening tea 6 1/2d, so that for the person taking all meals, the Board allowed a charge of 1/11d per day. For the six working days that would total 11/6d per week, which left the married worker with 12/6d per week to feed his wife and children, and to buy clothes, fuel, light and any other necessities.

A consideration of the official cost of keeping an inmate in county homes in 1936 will emphasize even more the position of labourers at the time. To provide an inmate with food, clothing and other necessities cost 7/6 in Sligo, 7/- in Carlow and 6/6 in Kildare. On that standard, a farm worker taking full board at his place of employment would find it very difficult to provide for more than his wife and one child (example cited in Labour Party **Annual Report**, 1937, p.162).

Nor did the Wages Board improve on that standard of living over the next eight years. While there was an 81.8% increase in farm wages from 22/- in 1937 to 40/3 in 1945, the cost of living during the same period rose by 74%, from an annual average index number of 160.25 to 294.5 (**Statistical Abstract**, 1947, p.195). Yet, during the same period, the agricultural price index increased for all products by an average of 90%, with both livestock products and crops doing well. Therefore, the bigger farmers who were the employers of labour were not required to pay increases equal to the amount by which their profits increased.

Average industrial earnings increased by only 29.6% during the 1937-45 period, mainly because of the Wages Standstill Order, 1941-6. Yet, even at that stage there was no narrowing of the gap between industrial and agricultural earnings. The average industrial wage increased by nearly 16/-, from 54/11 in 1938 to 70/8 in 1945, while the average farm wage increased by 13/- (ibid., 1945, p.202; 1952, p.110).

Government policy had a strong influence on the rate fixed by the Board during the first decade of its operations. It was more than a coincidence that the first rate established by the Board was 24/-. That also happened to be the sum paid by the government on relief schemes, and on work at the airport at Rinneanna.

More important was the fact that, from 1938 onwards, several government departments began to relate the rate of pay for their labourers directly to the Wages Board minimum, and hence had a vital interest in the rate determined by the Board. Labourers engaged on Land Commission improvement works, and those on Employment schemes, such as peat development and minor marine works, received the Wages Board rate in 1938 (SPO, S11689A, **Department of Finance Memo for the Government,** 1940, p.1). In addition, other classes in State employment were remunerated on the basis of a differential over and above the Board's minimum. They included drainage labourers, employed by the Commissioners of Public Works, and forestry labourers, employed by the Department of Lands (ibid.). Similarly, the wages of unskilled men on airport work at Rinneanna and Collinstown were increased by 3/- following increases of 3/- in the Board's prescribed minimum in May 1938. A few months earlier, the Parliamentary Secretary to the Minister for Finance had publicly linked the wages of airport and agricultural workers (Dail Debates, Vol 70, 9.3.1938). This was in fact a reversal of the procedure, noted earlier, for the year 1937, when the first Wages Board minimum was set at the going rate on airport work.

It was against the background of such linkage on pay that the Department of Finance sounded the alarm when the AWB announced in February 1940 that it proposed an increase of 3/- on the existing rate of 27/-. That Department reacted with a memorandum for the government on 28 February, 1940, in which it estimated that the new order would cost the government £70,000, consisting principally of £25,00 in respect of employment schemes, £22,00 on estate improvements, £10,000 on forestry, and £8,000 on airports (SPO, S11689A, **Department of Finance Memorandum for the Government,** 28.2.1940, p.3).

Since these increases could be given only "by imposing extra taxation or by retrenchment in numbers which would involve more unemployment", the Minister for Finance proposed that the linkage of state employee rates to AWB rates of pay, established two years earlier, should be broken, and no increase given to state employees. The cabinet endorsed the Minister's proposal, and no increase was given, except in the case of forestry labourers, on whose behalf the Department of Lands submitted a counter-memorandum. It informed the cabinet that "any attempt to withdraw the differential would be bound to meet with strong and reasoned opposition from the [forestry] labourers, who, in the past few years, have organised and have been pressing at various centres for higher wages and better working conditions" (SPO, S11689A, **Department of Lands Memorandum for the Government,** 28.2.1940, p.3).

The above material is introduced to indicate that even the modest increases granted by the AWB in its first four years of operation caused headaches for the government. Obviously, therefore, the government would not be anxious to see increases granted. But, as has also been demonstrated, a married farm worker with more than one child would have found it very difficult to survive even with the increases granted. Solving that problem, it seems, was not the government's priority. Rather did the pressure to restrict increases intensify.

In February 1942, the proposed amendment of Emergency Powers (No. 83) Order, 1941, was being considered, and it included provision for the resumption of the operations of the AWB. The Department of Local Government and Public Health warned the cabinet that:

> "In recent years there has been a considerable improvement in the wages of agricultural workers and at the present time the wages paid approximate to those of road workers in rural areas. In four counties the agricultural wage is in fact above the rural road wage. Any further increase in the wages of agricultural workers will affect the rates of wages paid by county councils to their workers, and if rural wages are increased it will mean an added burden on the rates, or a reduction in the extent of road works carried out. If the latter alternative should be adopted there would be an increase in uenmployment an a deterioration of the roads" (ibid., **Department of Local Government and Public Health memorandum for the Government,** 26.2.1942).

In the presence of such evidence, it is difficult to ignore the farm workers' claim that the government was putting covert pressure on the neutral members of the AWB to take the government's difficulties into account when determining a new rate. Indeed, the Minister for Local Government and Public Health thought so little of the autonomy of the AWB that he went as far as to demand from the cabinet in 1942 that the constitution of the Board be altered to permit him to be represented on it (ibid.).

Frustration on the workers' side at the lack of any significant progress under the AWB led to a revival of efforts at organisation towards the end of World War II.

The success of those efforts made the period 1946-50 a distinct one in the history of the AWB, because the fact that the unionized workers could apply considerable presure on the Board during those four years altered its decision-making process temporarily (see Chapter 5).

From 1950 onwards, government pressure on the Board was minimal, while the response of the Federation of Rural Workers to AWB increases was less militant. Thus, the internal decision making of the Board, and consequently the role of the independents, or 'neutral members', as they were officially designated, became more signficant once more. FRW members monopolized the worker positions on the Board after 1950. Patrick Murphy, Vice-President, and later President, of the FRW, served on the Board from 1949 to 1976. Con Moynihan, Cork County Chairman of the union from the inception of that branch in 1946, was a member from 1951 until 1976, while Patrick Durkan, Sligo County Secretary of the FRW, was on the Board from 1950 to 1966.

Even if the independents on the Board wished during the 1950s and 60s to make decisions by "averaging the recommendations of the Area Committees", as they had claimed to be doing in 1943, the reality was that matters of principle, such as the concept of a living wage, were constantly brought before the Board during the 1950s and 60s. Patrick Murphy, on behalf of both the workers' representatives on the Board and the FRW, submitted increasingly detailed and sophisticated memoranda, thus forcing the Board to give them serious consideration.

For example, for the 99th Meeting of the Board on 21 November, 1957, Murphy presented a Memorandum calling for a family wage for agricultural workers (copy in possession of members of AWB). This, he demanded, should be proportionate to the board and lodging allowances that agricultural employers were legally allowed to deduct from the wages of employees. He pointed out that, for food alone, farmers were allowed to retain 46% of weekly wages or 46/1d in Area A (Dublin), 44/11 in Area B (Kildare, Meath, Wicklow) and 43/9 in Area C (the remainder of the State). Murphy then calculated family food consumption on the basis of the Standard Scale normally used:

One male adult, 100% or one consumption unit.
One female adult, 83% of one consumption unit.
One juvenile, 10-14 years, 70% of one consumption unit.
One child, 5–9 years 60% of one consumption unit.
One child, under 5 years, 50% of one consumption unit.

For a family of five, comprising the above persons, the food bill per week would amount to 167/3 in Area A, 163/- in Area B, and 158/- in Area C. However, wages in those areas were only 106/-, 100/- and 95/- respectively, making it extremely difficult for the family to survive. It will be further noted that the preoccupation of spokesmen for the labourer in 1957 is a sufficient supply of food for the family, just what it had been twenty years before. That indicates the lack of improvement in the farm workers' standard of living over the years.

Nevertheless, neutrals and farmers alike remained unimpressed by such arguments and memoranda. The Board granted no increase in wages between May 1956 and May 1959. The independent members seemed more impressed by the fact that there was no increase in agricultural prices and farmer profits during these years.

The annual agricultural price index number, which stood at 98.7 in 1954 was 99.6 in 1960. But, in fact, this situation of apparently stagnating farm profits raises once more the two fundamental questions which were at the hub of farmer–worker bargaining: the necessity of distinguishing between the income of small and big farmers, and, secondly, the issue of a more equitable distribution of the farm cake, irrespective of its size.

With renewed emphasis on extensive farming during the 1950s, profits on the big farms, which was the sector employing wage labour, were much better than on small holdings. F.S.L. Lyons notes that "the best prices were obtained for the products of the bigger grass-farms while the increased price of feeding-stuffs adversely affected characteristic small-farm lines such as pigs and poultry" (**Ireland Since The Famine**, p.627).

The farm worker also could not help but notice how unskilled employees in other sectors continued to gain increases during the later 1950s. Average industrial wages increased from 153/8 in 1956 to 172/7 in 1959. This meant that the already wide gap of 56/11 between industrial and agricultural wages in 1956 was increased to 69/10 in 1959 (**Statistical Abstract**, 1956-9). Even more tangible for the farm worker was the enhanced position of his fellow rural workers. In March 1960, when farm workers were, on average, in receipt of 102/9, forestry labourers were getting 117/6d, road workers a minimum of 117/6, Bord na Mona employees 134/-, and ESB general workers 127/- (**Memo for AWB from P. Murphy, FRW, 10.3. 1960, Appendix 1**).

The publication of the interim reports of the National Farm Survey in 1958 and 1959 provided the workers' representatives on the Board with what seemed to them to be the evidence to copper-fasten their case for a substantial increase. They submitted a memorandum to the AWB on 10 March, 1960 with the challenge:

> "In the absence of authoritative evidence to the contrary, the AWB has no alternative but to accept the National Farm Survey as the best, and indeed the only guide to Farm Income and the distribution of employment. If any member of the Board has the slightest suspicion that agricultural income and employment is misrepresented in this memo, it is urged that the C.S.O. should be invited to clarify the findings of the National Farm Survey" (ibid., p.2).

That survey showed clearly that farms under fifty acres employed only an insignificant number of Male Hired Labour Units (a 'Unit' meaning fifty two weeks, or a 'man year'), while 65% of 50–100 acre farms employed no hired labour (ibid., Appendix 3). The volume of employment on those 29,000 farms over 100 acres equalled full-time employment for about 38,000 men, which left only 19,000 'man years' of employment for all the farms under 100 acres in size.

With regard to income the Survey showed that farms of 100–200 acres had a net weekly average income, clear of all expenses, including wages, of £26 15s, with those in the 30–50 acre range, by contrast, receiving £10 17 9d per week (ibid., Appendices 2 & 5). On the strength of these figures, workers' representatives on the AWB submitted that the farmers who employed labourers would have no difficulty in paying the minimum increase of 16/- per week demanded.

The other members of the Board were sceptical about the contents of the memorandum, and decided to submit it to the Central Statistics Office "to obtain the observations of that Office thereon" (**Letter from Secretary**, AWB to Director, CSO, 15.3.1960), and to request that an official from the CSO meet the Chairman and three other members of the Board, from the opposing sides, to discuss the matter.

The Director of the CSO, M.D. McCarthy, replied that it would be impossible to offer any observations or comment without dealing with the main problems raised, which were "primarily those of a social and economic nature which fall within the terms of reference of your Board" (**Letter from M.D. McCarthy** to Secretary, AWB, 29.3.1960, copy in possession of members of the Board). Furthermore, he pointed out, it was not appropriate that his Office should be put in a position where "its observations can be regarded as either directly supporting or opposing a case made by any sectional interest" (ibid.).

Thus, the outcome of several detailed submissions was that the independent members continued to ignore precise data during 1960 and gave an average increase of 7/- per week for that year, despite the case outlined above for a minimum increase of 16/-. At the beginning of 1961, therefore, the workers were more dissatisfied than ever. The Board meeting on 22 March, 1961 was presented with a letter from James Tully, Secretary, FRW, demanding an increase of 15/- per week. No decision was taken (**Minutes**, 112th Meeting, AWB, 22.3.1961, copy in possession of members of the Board).

When a Board meeting was held on 9 August, 1961, the advent of harvest added to the importance of agreement for both sides. The workers' representatives had lowered their demand to 10/- per week. In the course of heated exchanges at that meeting, it was revealed that at least three of the four main farmers' organisations — the National Farmers' Association and the Beef Producers' Association — were opposed to any increases whatever, on the grounds that entry to the Common Market was imminent, and "it would be unwise to take any steps that might jeopardise the farming industry until the effects of the Common Market were known" (**Dublin Evening Mail**, 10.8.1961). On hearing that argument, the workers' representatives walked out of the meeting and the FRW issued strike notice on behalf of its 5,000 members in counties Dublin, Meath and Kildare.

The Union also claimed that it could rely on similar action by the 46,000 permanent and 33,000 temporary labourers throughout the country. With the harvest "ripening quickly in the sun that followed the rain in the last few days" (ibid.), pressure was on the farmers. A strike was averted when they immediately entered negotiations with the FRW on an individual basis" (IT, 10.8.1961).

On 2 April, 1963, the worker members of the Board wrote to the Taoiseach, Sean Lemass: "We have with reluctance decided to inform you that we have now very little confidence in the AWB and we feel that we have no alternative but to ask you, as Head of the Government, to give us an opportunity of submitting a number of proposals which, we believe, would help to improve the position of the agricultural worker financially" (**Letter** from Patrick Murphy, FRW, on behalf of worker members, AWB, to Sean Lemass, 2.4.1963, copy in possession of members of AWB). The AWB continued to function as previously, however.

As national collective wage bargaining continued during the 1960s with the various Wage Rounds, the lesser increases granted by the Board each year were highlighted by the ICTU. During the period of Wage Round 11, 1968-69, for example, the Board granted 50/-, while the wages of forestry and drainage workers, and local authority employees of similar standing were increased by approximately 75/-. Against that background, a working party to examine the pay position of lower paid workers in the public service was set up by the government. It consisted of officers from the Departments of Finance, Post and Telegraphs, and Labour, and seven representatives of the Public Services Committee of the ICTU, one of whom was Patrick Murphy, the then President of the FRW.

While the position of the vast majority of farm workers obviously did not come within the brief of the working party, recommendations were made on pay increases for farm workers employed by the Department of Agriculture at its institutes (**Memo** submitted to AWB by P. Murphy, President, FRW, 6.4.1970, copy in possession of members of the AWB). In this way, the attention of the government was now brought directly to the role of the AWB and how it made its determinations, with the result that, at the meeting of the Board on 26 June, 1969, the chairman informed members that the Minister for Agriculture was in the process of setting up an inter-departmental Committee. Its terms of reference were:

> "to examine the legislation relating to the wages and holidays of agricultural workers and to report what changes, if any, should be made therein in the light of changing circumstances" (**Minutes**,152nd meeting, AWB, 26.6.69, copy in possession of members AWB).

Three years later, however, though the Committee had completed its report, matters were still at the stage where recommendations were being formulated for submission to the Minister for Agriculture "as to the extent to which the proposals in the Report might be accepted" (ibid., 167th meeting, 8.6.1972).

In the meantime, the signing of the Employer–Labour Conference National Agreement in December 1970 intensified even further the pressure on the AWB as the wage-fixing body that would not co-operate. Clause 3 of the Agreement provided for an increase of £2 per week in two phases over eighteen months (Letter from Employer–Labour Conference to AWB, 28.4.1972). By April 1972, the AWB had still only granted a total increase of £1.50. The FRW, whose President, Patrick Murphy, occupied a strategic position as ITUC member of the Employer-Labour Conference, complained about the AWB to the Steering Committee of that Conference (ibid.). The result was the first of what were to be many letters questioning the AWB from the Conference.

After the exchange of further letters (Employer-Labour Conference to AWB 21.7.1972; reply, 2.8.1972), the Joint Secretaries of the Employer–Labour Conference eventualy felt compelled, in September 1972, to point out that

> "if, for any reason, such a large and important section of employees as agricultural workers appeared to be unable to gain the full benefits of a National Pay Agreement, the whole concept of such Agreements would be seriously undermined" (Letter to AWB, 11.9.1972).

Six months later, however, the matter was still deadlocked. A letter from the Board to the Conference on 19 April, 1973 threw new light on the criteria to which the neutrals subscribed:

> "In discharging their statutory duty the Board would have regard to the National Agreements but it would be their responsibility also to take into account that some agricultural employers might not be able to pay wages above a certain level."

This was hardly sufficient cause for holding back on pay increases, however, and did not reflect well on the Board's decision making. As the Employer–Labour Conference replied

> "an unfortunate situation could be created if the vast majority of agricultural workers were to be deprived of increases laid down in the National Agreements because of the economic position of a small minority of the employers of such workers" (**Letter,** 28.6.73).

The AWB refused to yield. By the end of 1974, the Wages Board had made five orders failing to implement the National Agreement. The minimum wage stood at £24.80, when it would have been £27.42 had the National Agreement been granted. The AWB was eventually replaced by a Joint Labour Committee, under the *Industrial Relations Act*, 1976.

Conclusion

This study has set out to illustrate that farm labourers were a significant proportion of the Irish workforce up to the 1960s. The regional variations in the composition of the agricultural workforce were emphasised to highlight the fact that labourers were concentrated in twelve Leinster and Munster counties. There were people in Ireland materially worse off than farm labourers during the twentieth century, and these included some 'farmers' and their relatives assisting. The small farmers, however, were for the most part west of the Dundalk–Limerick City–Bandon lines. While some labourers had a higher standard of living than some small farmers, the labour felt his *social status* to be inferior to the property owner's, however little land the small farmer owned. Furthermore, it was with the big farmer who employed workers that the labourer contrasted his position, rather than with the small farmer.

Relations were frequently bad between employing farmers and labourers, and, during the twentieth century, this came to the surface when the World Wars altered the economic parameters governing agriculture, thus presenting the labourers with a degree of leverage. Before 1916, the labourers' strategy had been political agitation for the most part. The various factions of the Land and Labour Associations were the vehicles for political activity.

In 1917, the establishment of the Agricultural Wages Board gave the signal for trade union rather than political agitation. The ensuing struggle between the LLAs and the ITGWU for the loyalty of farm workers therefore had a political dimension. The LLAs were in the Home Rule camp, while the ITGWU had been firmly in the republican fold since James Connolly had led the Citizen Army into the GPO.

Trade Union agitation on the farm was successful in 1919-20 because economic prosperity enabled farmers to pay, while the withdrawal of the RIC from the countryside left employers vulnerable to the obstruction of pickets. The nature of farming was such that the effects of picketing would be felt very quickly. In addition, trade union agitation re-awakened the long tradition of agrarian violence in rural Ireland. This had been used by both farmers and labourers against landlords for 150 years, and now labourers employed it against big farmers. While the trade union did not condone agrarian crime, it could not control the excesses of farm workers. The relationship was in ways similar to that between Parnell and 'Captain Moonlight'.

In 1921, the economic conditions reverted to the pre-war position, with the advent of economic recession and consequent unemployment. Farm workers became conscious of the reserve labour pool in the countryside once more, while employing farmers began to demand wage reductions because of falling prices. The abolition of the Agricultural Wages Board, along with guaranteed prices for corn in June 1921, was a severe blow to the labourers' position.

Henceforth, the trade union branch was the only lawful defence against wage reductions. Strikes became increasingly bitter as the stakes became higher.

The final phase of the Anglo-Irish war severely restricted labour agitation, but at the same time the tension between employing farmer and worker ran very high and was scarcely concealed. The present study provides further evidence in support of recent works which have exposed the myth of nationalist solidarity and unity during the Anglo-Irish War.

Indeed, the farm workers openly adopted the slogans, emblems, and rhetoric of socialism, which greatly alarmed "conservative republicans". However, an analysis of the labourers' enthusiasm for the Red Flag and "Bolshevism" indicates that militant trade unionism of the Larkinite variety, rather than revolutionary socialism, was what motivated rural workers.

The eleven months between the Truce and Civil War saw a strong revival in militant trade unionism, but the Civil War wreaked havoc in the agricultural sector once more. By January 1923, the Free State government was in a position to clamp down on any agitation that threatened law and order. Accordingly, agricultural trade unionism was suppressed because union agitation was associated with agrarian crime, in the view of the Free State government.

There was no revival of trade unionism on the farm until 1943. Appropriately enough, it was Jim Larkin who initiated the re-organisation. The years 1944 to 1948 saw a vigorous union campaign for a weekly half-day and a week's paid annual holidays, which most other full-time workers in the state enjoyed by 1940. Labourer agitation was made the focus of a Red scare in 1946-7.

An examination of the period, 1924-36, when there was no trade union involvement or government intervention in the agricultural sector, reveals a declining standard of living for many farm workers. Some farmers continued to offer good pay and working conditions, but others took advantage of the laissez-faire position. Government intervention in 1936, with the re-introduction of the AWB, improved matters from the workers' viewpoint to a limited extent. The amount of arrears recovered by the AWB in its first eight years of operation, and the volume of requests registered for visits by inspectors of the Board, suggests the extent of difficulties for employees prior to 1936. However, the AWB's procedural machinery and the absence from its constitution of definite guidelines for the independent members retarded performance.

One hundred years after the Famine, the descendants of the class which suffered most from that catastrophe were engaged in a bitter struggle in Kildare, which witnessed activities on all sides more appropriate to the famine era than mid-20th century Ireland. As a consequence of the Famine, agricultural labourers became a disadvantaged minority, rather than a disadvantaged majority. After 1850, they suffered the fate that often befalls minorities. However, their militancy when the opportunity presented itself, as in 1919-23 and 1946-7, suggests that, had their numbers not been decimated by the Famine, the subsequent history of Ireland would indeed have been different.

Review Of Sources

Primary Sources

For the introductory chapter, the **Census of Population**, 1911, 1926, 1936, 1951, and 1966 provided most material on the numerical strength, regional location, age and conjugal status of labourers. The **Report of the Commission on Emigration and other Population Problems** (1954) supplemented the census material. The **Parliamentary Debates of Dail Eirean** (Dail Debates) 1922–62 provided useful statistical and background material on labourers' cottages and legislation related to farm labourers.

The **Limerick Rural Survey**, Third Interim Report (Tipperary 1962) was a sociological survey of class structure, which provided very useful material on the social status of farm workers, and the relationship between employing farmer and labourer. It was supplemented by Pat Feeley's **Servant boys and girls in Co. Limerick**, *Old Limerick Journal*, i, (December 1979), p.32-6). Feeley worked as a teacher in the East Limerick/West Tipperary border area in the early 1960s, where he noted a "searing class division". His work, at any rate, is useful as first hand observation. The **National Nutrition Survey** provided a comprehensive and objective investigation of the diet of farm workers' families, and contrasted it with other social groupings.

Having established this broad outline, it was decided to undertake a survey of fifty agricultural labourers, over the age of fifty. However, a pilot survey of ten men suggested that more fruitful results would emerge from written sources, which those interviews pin-pointed. The danger of imbalance consequent on not interviewing an equal number of employing farmers was also noted. Subsequent interviews with four farmers indicated that the employing farmer's viewpoint during the twentieth century could be culled from farmers' newspapers.

It emerged from interviews with the ten labourers that Con Moynihan, MCC of Carrigrohane, Co. Cork, had been a leading spokesman for labourers for many years. Accordingly, Mr. Moynihan was approached, and proved an invaluable source. He was more than generous with interviews and his extensive source material. Mr. Moynihan had been a founder member of the Federation of Rural Workers in Cork, served as county chairman of the FRW, 1946–1950, and was a member of the *central* Agricultural Wages Board for the long period, 1951-1976.

Mr. Moynihan also pointed to Patrick Murphy, Vice-President, FRW during the 1950s, and then President of the FRW until 1979, when it merged with the WUI to form the FWUI. In addition, Mr. Murphy was a member of the AWB, 1947-76. Mr. Murphy kindly granted time from his busy work schedule in Dublin and Brussels for an interview, and then generously provided copies of manuscript material from a file on the early years of the FRW. Those manuscripts are at present stored at FWUI Head Office, 29 Parnell Square, Dublin 1.

The Department of Labour, Davitt House, Waterloo Road, Dublin 4, provided useful memoranda published by the AWB, 1937-76. The Dail Report, Vol 64, November 1936 contains the debates on the *Agricultural Wages Bill*. These run to over 100 pages and all aspects of the labourer question were discussed. The Minister for Agriculture, Dr.

Ryan, provided very useful statistical data during the debate on variations in labourers' wages, the distribution of agricultural income, and the size of holdings which employed labourers, as distinct from farmers and their families.

The State Paper Office, Dublin Castle, holds valuable files on departmental memoranda for the Cabinet (Executive Council) on the proposed AWB in 1936, and confidential memoranda on the functioning of the Board after that date. In addition, the reports of the chairman, AWB, to the Minister for Agriculture are available for the years 1937-1947 at the State Paper Office. They provide valuable information on the Board's activities in relation to inspection, recovery of arrears, prosecutions, interviews and the granting of exemption permits to incapacitated workers.

Newspaper material proved to be extensive on the farm strikes of 1946-7. The **Irish Times** was consulted to trace the growth of the WUI among farm labourers, 1944-6. In addition, the **Irish Press** was consulted for the North Kildare farm strike, August-September 1946. The **Standard** contained much anti-labourer material during the North Kildare strike, while the opposing viewpoint was presented in the **Irish People**, official organ of the Irish Labour Party. This weekly newspaper also proved useful for details of farm disputes, 1947-8.

A preliminary study indicated that the years of the first AWB, 1917-21, would repay intensive study on a county basis. Cork was then made the focus of such a study. A reading of the **Cork Examiner** for 1917 revealed that several rural Land and Labour factions existed. These were then traced backwards by means of the Examiner, which gave extensive coverage to the ILLA up to 1905, because the latter was aligned to the Home Rule Party and United Irish League, and George Crosbie, proprietor of the Examiner, had himself been a Home Rule MP. The ILLA split in two in 1905 and thereafter the anti-William O'Brien/D.D. Sheehan faction got the support of the Examiner, while the viewpoint of the other faction is presented in newspapers associated with William O'Brien. These include **Cork Weekly News**, 1905, **North Cork Herald**, 1906, **Cork Free Press** and **Cork Accent**, 1910. D.D. Sheehan's **Ireland Since Parnell** (London 1920) provides the same viewpoint as those newspapers.

Most effort and attention in this research was devoted to the intensive study of the years 1918–23. The **Examiner** was read in its entirety for those years, and provided detailed material on the waves of farm strikes, agrarian violence and political upheaval. The Nationalist and conservative tendencies of the Examiner were balanced by a reading of the official organs of farmers and labourers. The ITGWU position was presented in **Irish Opinion,** December 1917-April 1918; **Voice of Labour,** April 1918–September 1919, **Watchword of Labour,** September 1919–December 1920, and **Voice of Labour,** November 1921-1925. Mr. Liam Beecher, secretary, Cork No. 6 Branch, ITGWU, kindly made available his own published articles on Tadg Barry and the early years of the ITGWU in Cork.

The William O'Brien (trade unionist) collection, MSS 13906–79 and 15650–712 in the National Library of Ireland, contains useful material on Cork, in addition to the census of membership, 30.6.1918. MS7282 ITGWU NLI is an indexed list of branches, 1919-22.

The **Irish Farmer**, September 1919–August 1922, was the organ of the Irish Farmers' Union. The **Farmers' Gazette** represented Cork Farmers' Union, and the Irish Dairy Shorthorn Breeders' Society. It incorporated the **Irish Farming World**, and after 1922, the **Irish Farmer**. While used extensively up to 1923, the **Farmers' Gazette** was also used to trace the views of farmers, 1923-40. The organs of the farming co-operative movement — the Irish Agricultural Organisation Society (IAOS) — were also used extensively to get an appreciation of the attitudes of the farming community and the problems facing farmers. The newspapers were **The Irish Homestead**, 1895–1923, which for many years had the added attraction of AE (George Russell) as editor. It was replaced by **The Irish Statesman**, 1923-30, and then **Agricultural Ireland**, 1941-62.

Other newspapers used for the 1930s were **Labour News**, 1936-38, which presented the labourers' response to the introduction of the AWB, the **Irish Independent** for the same period, and **Irish Workers' Weekly** (1939-41).

Agricultural journals also proved useful for an overview of developments. Those used included the **Journal of Department of Agriculture and Technical Instruction** (DATII), 1900–1918; and **Journal of the Department of Agriculture**, 1924-40. **Annual Reports** which proved useful were those of the Department of Agriculture, 1921-43; ITGWU, 1918-50; ITUC 1894-1911, 1930-45; Irish Labour Party and Trade Union Congress, 1918-29; Irish Labour Party, 1930-40.

The **Report of the Commission on Agriculture**, 1924, was very important as a statement of Free State Policy on Agriculture, while George O'Brien's article on Patrick Hogan in **Studies**, XXV, 1936, analyses (from an admirer's viewpoint) the policy of the first Free State Minister for Agriculture.

Broadcast material which proved informative on hiring fairs and servant boys and girls included **Folklands**, presented by Seamus O'Catháin, RTE Radio 1, 10.4.83, 4.3.84, 11,3,84; **Women Today**, presented by Phil Crotty, RTE Radio 1, 14.4.82; and **Looking South**, presented by Dan Collins, RTE Radio 1, 31.5.84.

Secondary Sources

David Fitzpatrick, **The disappearance of the Irish Agricultural Labourer, 1841-1912**, *Irish Economic and Social History*, vii, 1980, p.66-92, provides a wealth of statistical data and analysis, and stresses the pitfalls of trying to distinguish between small farmer and labourer. John W. Boyle's article, **A Marginal Figure: The Irish Rural Labourer**, in Samuel Clark and James S. Donnelly, Jr. (eds) **Irish Peasants: Violence and Political Unrest 1780–1914** (Manchester 1983), provides some useful material on housing, but is for the most part an updating of Boyle's article, **The Rural Labourer**, *Threshold*, iii, no. 1 (Spring 1959). Padraig G. Lane's **The Agricultural Labourer in Ireland 1850-1914**, unpublished Ph.D thesis (UCC), NUI, 1980, provides a good account of the Irish Land and Labour Association up to 1906.

In recent years, a good deal of material on labourers during the 1917-23 period has appeared. C. Desmond Greaves, **The Irish Transport and General Workers' Union: The Formative Years 1909–23** (Dublin 1982) is very useful for union background material, though short on footnotes. David Fitzpatrick's **Politics and Irish Life 1913-21: Provincial Experience of War and Revolution** (Dublin 1977) deals, among many other themes, with labourers in Clare, and also contains a very good bibliography. Emmet O'Connor's **Agrarian Unrest and the Labour Movement in Co. Waterford 1917–23**, *Saothar*, vi (1980), p.40-58, gives an excellent account of the 1923 strike in Waterford.

Finally, Howard Newby, **The Deferential Worker, A Study of Farm Workers in East Anglia** (London 1977) provided a useful comparison for Britain.

Bibliography

1. Manuscript Material

MSS Con Moynihan: manuscripts relating to Mr. Moynihan's years as Cork County Secretary, FRW, 1946–50, and years of membership of AWB, 1951-76. In his possession, Carrigrohane, Co. Cork.

MSS Patrick Murphy: manuscripts relating to the early years of the FRW. Located at Head Office, FWUI, 29 Parnell Square, Dublin 1.

National Library of Ireland (NLI): ITGWU indexed list of branches, 1909-22, with typed list of branch membership 1918, MS 7282.

NLI: William O'Brien (ITGWU) collection. MSS 13906-79.

NLI: Redmond Papers, MSS 15182-7.

State Paper Office (SPO): Memoranda relating to the proposed AWB, 1936, S8744.

SPO: First Report of Chairman, AWB, to Minister for Agriculture, S11689.

SPO: Reports of Chairman, AWB, to Minister for Agriculture, 1940-47. S8744, S13503[A].

SPO: Memoranda for Government on functioning of AWB, 1940-47. S11689[A], S11689[B].

SPO: Memoranda for Government on proposed amendment of *Agricultural Wages Act*, 1936, 1944. S13296.

2. Official Publications

Agricultural Statistics 1847-1926, Stationery Office (SO), 1930.
Agricultural Statistics 1927-1933, SO 1935.
Agricultural Statistics 1934-1956, SO 1960.
Agricultural Wages Board, memoranda of, 1937-76.
Census of Population 1911, 1926, 1936, 1946, 1951, 1961, 1966.
Department of Agriculture, Annual Reports of, 1921-43.
Department of Agriculture, Journal of, 1924-40.
Emigration and other Population Problems, Report of Commission on, SO 1954.
Irish Trade Journal, 1925-.
Journal of Department of Agriculture and Technical Instruction for Ireland, 1900-14.
Journal of Department of Agriculture, 1924-40.
National Farm Survey, 1955-6, 1957-8, SO.
National Nutrition Survey 1946-8, SO 1953.
Report of Commission on Agriculture, SO 1924.
Report of Commission on Vocational Organisation (Chairman: Bishop Michael Browne), SO 1943.

3. Parliamentary Debates

Parliamentary Debates, Dail Eireann, 1922-64.

4. Other Reports

ITGWU Annual Reports 1918-50.
ITUC Annual Reports 1894-1911, 1930-45.
ILPTUC Annual Reports 1918-29.
Labour Party Annual Reports 1930-40.
Limerick Rural Survey, Third Interim Report, Tipperary 1962.

5. Newspapers And Periodicals

Agricultural Ireland 1941-62.
Cork Accent 1910.
Cork Examiner 1917-23, 1946-48.
Cork Free Press 1912.
Cork Weekly News 1905-9.
Farmers' Gazette 1917-20.
Freeman's Journal 1890, 1894.
Irish Farmer 1919-22.
Irish Homestead 1910-23.
Irish Independent 1917, 1935-37.
Irish Times 1917-20, 1936, 1944-47.
Irish Opinion 1917-18
Irish People 1905-06, 1946-48.
Irish Press 1946-48.
Irish Statesman 1923-30
Irish Worker 1913.
Irish Workers' Weekly 1937-41.
Labour News 1936-38.
North Cork Herald 1906.
Standard 1946.
United Ireland 1890, 1894.
Voice of Labour 1918-19, 1921-24.
Watchword of Labour 1919-20.
West Cork Eagle 1881.

6. Personal Interviews

Con Moynihan: 23.2.1982; 2.4.1982.
Patrick Murphy: 19.7.84.

7. Broadcast Material

Folklands presented by Seamus O Catháin, RTE Radio 1, 10.4.83, 4.3.84, 11.3.84.
Women Today presented by Phil Crotty, RTE Radio 1, 14.4.82.
Looking South presented by Dan Collins, RTE Radio 1, 31.5.84.

B. *Secondary Sources*

1. CONTRIBUTIONS TO JOURNALS

J.W. BOYLE, "The Rural Labourer", in *Threshold*, iii, no.1 (Spring 1959), 29-40.

PATRICK CAMPBELL, "A Man from the Croaghs Remembers", in *Donegal Annual*, viii, no. 1 (1969), 109-15.

PAT FEELEY, "Servant Boys and Girls in Co. Limerick", in *Old Limerick Journal*, i, (1979), 32-6.

DAVID FITZPATRICK, "The Disappearance of the Agricultural Labourer 1814-1912", in *Irish Economic and Social History*, vii (1980), 66-92.

DAVID FITZPATRICK, "Strikes in Ireland, 1914-21", in *Saothar*, vi (1980), 26-38.

P.L.R. HORN, "The National Agricultural Labourers' Union in Ireland 1873-9", in *IHS*, xvii, no. 67 (March 1971), 340-52.

RICHARD HAWKINS, Review of Captain Swing, by E.J. Hobsbawm and George Rude, *IHS*, xvii, no. 67 (Sept 1969), 525-6.

K.T. HOPPEN, "Landlords, Society and Electoral Politics in Mid-Nineteenth Century Ireland", in *Past and Present*, no 75 (May 1977), 62-95.

JOURNAL OF THE STATISTICAL AND SOCIAL INQUIRY SOCIETY OF IRELAND (JSSISI), 1900-1960, passim.

R.J. KELLY, "The Agricultural Labourers of Ireland", in *New Ireland Review*, xx (1903), 297-310.

EDWARD E. MacLYSAGHT, "Some Thoughts on the Rural Labour Question", in *Irish Monthly*, xlvii (1919), 575-93.

GEORGE O'BRIEN, "Patrick Hogan", in *Studies*, xxv (Sept 1936), 353-68.

EMMET O'CONNOR, "Agrarian Unrest and the Labour Movement in County Waterford, 1917-23", in *Saothar*, vi (1980), 40-58.

BOB ROCKETT, "Skilled Labour on the Farm", in *Waterford Plough and Furrow*, ii, no. 2 (1954), 14.

2. THESES

PADRAIG G. LANE, "The Agricultural Labourer in Ireland 1850-1914", (Ph.D Thesis, UCC, 1980).

EMMET O'CONNOR: "The Politics of the Labour Movement in County Waterford since 1890", (UCG, MA Thesis 1979).

3. BOOKS

ARENSBERG, C.M. and KIMBALL, S.T., "Family and Community in Ireland", (2nd ed, Cambridge, Mass., 1968).

BEW, P., "Land and the National Question in Ireland, 1858-82", (Dublin 1978).

BOYLE, J.W., "Leaders and Workers", (Cork, 1966).

BOYLE, J.W., "A Marginal Figure: The Irish Rural Labourer" in Clarke, S. and Donnelly, J.S. Jr. (eds), "Irish Peasants: Violence and Political Unrest, 1780-1914", (Manchester, 1983).

CHUBB, B., "The Government and Politics of Ireland", (London 1970).

CLARKE, S., "Social Origins of the Irish Land War", (Princetown 1979).

CLARKE S., "The Importance of Agrarian Classes: Agrarian Structure and Collective Action in Nineteenth Century Ireland" in P.J. Drudy (ed) "Irish Studies 2. Ireland: Land, Politics and People", (Cambridge 1982).

CLARKSON, J.D., "Labour and Nationalism in Ireland", (New York 1925).

CONNELL, K.H., "Irish Peasant Society", (Oxford 1968).

CONNOLLY, J., "Labour in Irish History", (Dublin 1910).

CONNOLLY, J., "The Reconquest of Ireland", (Dublin 1917).

CONNOLLY, J., "The Worker's Republic" — a selection of the writings of James Connolly, with an introduction by Desmond Ryan, (Dublin 1951).

CONNOLLY, J., "Socialism and Nationalism" — a selection of the writings of James Connolly, with an introduction by Desmond Ryan, (Dublin 1948).

CROTTY, R., "Irish Agricultural Production: Its Volume and Structure", (Cork 1966).

DALY, S., "Cork: a City in Crisis", (Cork 1978).

DANAHER, K., "Irish Country People", (Cork 1969).

DAVITT, M., "The Fall of Feudalism in Ireland", (London and New York, 1904).

DEENY, J., "The Irish Worker: a demographic study of the workforce in Ireland", (Dublin 1971).

DONNELLY, J.S., Jr., "The Land and the People of Nineteenth Century Cork: the rural economy and the land question" (London and Boston, 1975).

DRUDY, P.J. (ed), "Irish Studies 2. Ireland: Land, Politics and People", (Cambridge 1982).

FARLEY, D., "Social Insurance and Social Assistance in Ireland", (Dublin 1964).

FITZPATRICK, D., "Class, Family and Rural Unrest in Nineteenth Century Ireland", in "Irish Studies 2. Ireland: Land, Politics and People", (Cambridge 1982).

FITZPATRICK, D., "Politics and Irish Life 1913-21: Provincial Experience of War and Revolution", (Dubln 1977).

FREEMAN, T.W., "Ireland: its Physical, Historical, Social and Economic Geography", (London 1950).

GREAVES, C.D., "The Life and Times of James Connolly", (Dublin 1961).

GREAVES, C.D., "Liam Mellows and the Irish Revolution" (London 1961).

GREAVES, C.D., "The Irish Transport and General Workers' Union The Formative Years 1909-23" (Dublin 1982).

HANNAN, D., "Rural Exodus", (London 1970).

HOBSBAWM, E.J. and RUDE, G., "Captain Swing", (London 1970).

ITGWU, "Fifty Years of Liberty Hall 1909-59", (Dublin 1959).

KENNEDY, R.E., "The Irish: Emigration, Marriage and Fertility", (Berkley, 1973).
KEOGH, D., "The Rise of the Irish Working Class", (Dublin 1982).
LARKIN, E., "James Larkin, Irish Labour Leader 1876-1947", (London, 1965).
LEE, J., "The Ribbonmen", in T.D. Williams (ed), "Secret Societies in Ireland", (Dublin and New York 1973).
LEE, J., "The Modernisation of Irish Society 1848-1918", (Dublin 1973).
LYND, R., "Home Life in Ireland", (Dublin 1909).
LYONS, F.S.L., "John Dillon", (London 1968).
LYONS, F.S.L., "The Irish Parliamentary Party 1890-1910", (Connecticut 1975).
LYONS, F.S.L., "Ireland Since the Famine", (Revised ed, London 1973).
MxCARTHY, C., "Trade Unions in Ireland, 1894-1960", (Dublin 1977).
McCARTHY, M.J.F., "Irish Land and Irish Liberty", (Dublin 1911).
MacGILL, P., "Children of the Dead End", (London 1912).
McGILVRAY, J., "Irish Economic Statistics", (Dublin 1968).
MEENAN, J., "The Irish Economy since 1922", (Liverpool 1957).
MITCHELL, A., "Labour in Irish Politics 1890-1930", (Dublin 1979).
MURPHY, J.A., "Ireland in the Twentieth Century" (Dublin 1975).
NEVIN, D., "Trade Unions and Change in Irish Society, (Dublin 1980).
NEWBY, H., "The Deferential Worker: A Study of Farm Workers in East Anglia", (London 1977).
O'BRIEN, J.V., "William O'Brien and the Course of Irish Politics", (Berkley, 1976).
O'BRIEN, W., "Forth the Banners Go, Reminiscences of William O'Brien as told to Edward MacLysaght", (Dublin 1969).
O'CONNOR-LYSAGHT, R.D., "The Republic of Ireland", (Cork 1970).
O'DOWD, A., "Meitheal — A Study of Co-operative Labour in Rurual Ireland", (Dublin 1981).
O'DONNELL, P., "Adrigoole" (London l929).
O'NEILL, B., "The Struggle for the Land in Ireland", (London 1934).
O'SHEA, J., "Priests, Politics and Society in Post Famine Ireland — A Study of Co. Tipperary 1850-91", (Dublin 1983).
O'TUATHAIGH, M.A.G., "The Land Question, Politics and Irish Society 1922-1960", in P.J. Drudy (ed), "Irish Studies 2. Ireland: Land, Politics and People", (Cambridge 1982).
PAUL-DUBOIS, L., "Contemporary Ireland", (Dublin 1908).
RUMPF, E. and HEPBURN, A.C., "Nationalism and Socialism in Twentieth Century Ireland", (Liverpool 1977).
SHEEHAN, D.D., "Ireland Since Parnell", (London 1920).
THOMPSON, F., "Lark Rise to Candleford" (Penguin Modern Classics ed. Hammondsworth, 1973).
TONER, J., "Rural Ireland: Some of its Problems", (Dublin 1955).
VAN VORIS, J., Constance de Markievicz in the Service of Ireland", (Amherst Mass., 1967).
WILLIAMS, T.D. (ed), "Secret Societies of Ireland" (Dublin and New York, 1973).
WOLF, E.R., "Peasant Wars of the Twentieth Century", (London 1971).

Index

"Adrigoole" (Peadar O'Donnell), 15
Aghada 'Red Guards', 54-55
— 1921 Strike, 59
Agricultural Wages Board (AWB), 8, 16, 17, 20, 34, 36, 42, 43, 74, 75, 89-90, 91, 92, 117, 188, Ch. 6 *passim*
— Abolition of, 1921, 58
— Area Committees, 105, 106, 107
— Chairman, Powers of, 106-7
— Composition of, 104-5
— Independent Member, Role, 108-9, 111, 114
— Inspectors of, 102-3
— Government influence on, 110
— Performance of, 109-16
— Results of intervention, 1937-45, 103
All-For-Ireland League, 29
Arch, Joseph, 24
Association of Rural Workers and Workmen's Labour Unions, 35
Athy, 78
— Farm Strike, 1923, 65, 66-67, 72, 78

Baird, James, 69
Ballincollig, 28, 36, 51
— 1922 Strike, 63
— FRW Branch, 88
Ballingarry Farm Strike, 1923, 67-68, 72
Ballinhassig, 24
Ballybricken, 69
Ballygarvan, 52
Ballyline (Ballingarry) Strike, 1923, 67-68
Bandon, 8, 10, 11
Barry, Tadg(h), 34, 42, 47, 48, 51-52
— Killing of, 57, 62
Barry, Tom, 57
Bartlemy (Near Fermoy), 61, 64, 70-71

Black and Tans, 52, 54, 56, 57
Blarney, ILLA, 36
— ITGWU, 34
Beef Producers' Association, 114
Belton, Patrick, 77
Bennett, Louie, 78, 81
Bishopstown, 64
— ILLA, 36
— ITGWU, 36, 51
— 1922 Farm Strike, 63
Board of Guardians, 21
Bradley, Patrick, 28, 29, 30, 32, 33, 36, 41, 42
Brady, M.J., 80
Buckley, Cornelius, 26, 33, 36, 37
Buckley, Patrick, 44
Budget, A Labourer's, 1923, 13
Bulgaden, 1921 Strike, 61-62
'Bunclody Agreement', 35
Butler, John, TD, 68-69
Butt, Isaac, 25
Buttevant, 47, 54

Cairns, P.J., 78, 81
Campbell, J.R., 95
Carew, Lord, 82
Carlow, Co., 8, 11, 22
Carrigrohanebeg, 28, 30
Cashel Archdiocese, 13
Castlemagner, 30
Castletownroche, 52
Cavan, Co., 10, 20, 22
Cave Committee on Trade Boards, 108
Celbridge, 45
— 'Siege of', 1946, 83-84
Central Harvesting Bureau, 86
Central Statistics Office, 114
Charleville, 13, 24
— ITGWU Branch, 43
"Children of the Dead End", 16

Churchtown Labour League, 34
— Shooting Incident, 47
— 1920 Farm Strike, 54
Citizen's Army, 117
Civil War, 8, 56, 63-64, 65, 71, 118
Clare, Co., 10, 22, 27
Cloghroe ITGWU Branch, 44
Collingstown Airport Scheme, 110
Commission on Agriculture, Report, 1924, 93-95
Conditions of Employment Act 1936, 17, 74
Congress of Irish Unions, 79
Connolly, James, 117
Conroy, John, 79
Contract System, One Year, 16
Corish, Brendan, 90, 91
Cork, Co., 8, 9, 11, 15, 16, 21, 22, 24, 27
— Farm Strikes, 1919, 49
— Farm Strikes, 1920, 53
— Threatened Farm Strikes, 1919, 50
— Wage Rates in 1931 & 1935, 97-98
Cork Farmers' Asociation, 89
Cork Farmers' Union, 51, 59
Corn Production Act 1917 (AWB), 34, 104
— Repeal of, 58
Cottages, 11, 20, 21, 28
Cumann Na nGaedheal, 93-94, 102

Davitt, Michael, 26
Day, Bob, 60, 64
Dease, E.J., 82
Delgany, Wicklow, Dispute, 1947, 91
Democratic Trade and Labour Federation, 26
Desmond, Dan, 16, 88, 89, 91
de Valera, Eamon, 86
Diet, Labourers', 13-15
Dillon, James, 92, 101
Dillon, John, 27
Donegal, Co., 10, 22
Doneraile, 52
Doughcloyne, 54
Dublin Agricultural Association, 77
Dublin Co., 8, 11, 12, 22
— 1922 Strike, 62
— 1923 Strike, 65
— 1946 Strike, 80

Duffy, Michael, 94
Duhallow Trade and Labour Association, 26
Duignan, John, 81
Dunne, Sean, 78-92 *passim*
Durkan, Patrick, 112

Emergency Powers (No. 83) Order 1941, 111
Employer-Labour Conference, 17, 115-16

Factories and Shops Act 1896, 104
Farmers' Flying Column, 67, 82
Farmers' Freedom Force, 51
"Farmers' Gazette", 100
Federation of Rural Workers (FRW), 8, 16, 17, 20, 106, 112, Ch. 5 *passim*
— Membership Figures, 1947, 87
— Cork Branch, 87-90
— North Kildare Strike, 1946, 82-87
Feeley, Pat, 15
Fenor, Co. Waterford, 69
— 'Battle of', 46
Fermoy, 13, 64
— ITGWU Branch, 41, 71
Finance, Department of, Memorandum, 1936, 100-101
— Memo, 1940, 110-111
Fianna Fáil, 104, 105
Fine Gael, 102
Foran, Thomas, 33, 34, 35, 100

"Gallybally Farmer", 15n
Gurtroe (Near Youghal) Strike, 1921, 61

Hallisey, Tim, 88
Harte, E.P., 81
Hayden, Thomas, 90
Hennigan, Commandant, 62
Hiring Fairs, 15-16
Hogan, Patrick, Minister for Agriculture, 93
Holidays Act 1939, 17, 74
Holidays Act, Agricultural Workers 1950, 91
— Weekly Half-Holidays Act 1952, 92
Housing, Labourers', 20-23

Houston, Denis, 34, 37
Hunter, Thomas, TD, 52
Hurley, Jeremiah, TD, 105

Independent Landless League, 70
Industrial Relations Act 1946, 17, 87
Industrial Relations Act 1976, 17, 116
Inniscarra Farmers' Union, 48
Inniscarra ITGWU Branch, 47
Insurance Commissioners, Irish, 18
Irish Congress of Trade Unions, 115
Irish Farmers' Union, 51, 61
"Irish Farmer", 61
Irish Land and Labour Association, 8, 26, 27, 30, 31, 32, 33, 34, 105, 117
— Split in, 27-28, 32-33
— Cork Co. LLA, 28
— Cork City and Co. LLA, 29
— Membership of AWB, 32-33
— Competition with ITGWU, 35-42
— Mogeely Branch, 42
— Queenstown Branch, 32
— South Kilmurry Branch, 37, 41
— Youghal Branch, 37
Irish National Trade and Labour League, 35
"Irish People", 85
Irish Republican Army (IRA), 56, 60-61, 62
Irish Seamen's and Port Workers' Union, 85
Irish Trade and Labour League, 105
Irish Trade Union Congress, 79, 100
Irish Transport and General Workers' Union (ITGWU), 8, 13, 15, 31, 33, 105, 117, Chs. 3 & 4 *passim*
— Competition with ILLA, 35-42
— Census of Membership, 1920, 43
— Number Farm Labourers in Cork Branches, 56
— Destruction of Rural Branches, 56
— Role of Rural Branch Secretary, 1918-23, 70-72
— Big Branch Scheme, 71
— Blarney Branch, 65
— Buttevant Branch, 64
— Shanballymore Branch, 63

Johnson, Phillip F., 24-25
Johnson, Thomas, 59, 79, 81, 94
Joint Labour Committee (Agricultural Workers), 17, 116

Kanturk, 8, 11, 24, 25, 34
— Egmont Arms Hotel, 25
— Labourers' Club, 24
— Trade and Labour Association, 26
Kavanagh, James, 83
Kerry, Co., 10, 15, 22, 27
Kilavullen, 52
Kildare, Co., 8, 11, 22
— North Kildare Strike, 1946, 74, 82-87, 118
— South Kildare Strike, 1947, 91
Kildare Farmers' Association, 82, 83, 86
Kildare Farmers' Union, 45
Kilkea, South Kildare, 78
Kilkenny, Co., 8, 11, 12, 22
Kilmallock, 15, 62
— Incident, 45
Kilmanagh (Ballingarry), 1923 Strike, 67-68
Kilmeaden, Co. Waterford, 68
Kilmichael Ambush, 57
Kilmurry South, 52

Labour Court, 17, 87, 90
— Recommendation on Farm Workers' Holidays, 1947, 90
Labourers' Acts, 7, 21, 22, 26, 28
Labour League, 25
Labour Party, 101
'Lady Day', 25th March, 21, 36, 59, 63, 65
Lands, Department of, Memorandum, 1940, 111
Langan, T.J., 79, 80, 81
Larkin, Jim, 8, 33-34, 71, 75, 76, 78, 79, 80, 81, 88, 90, 118
Larkin, Jim, Jnr., 75, 78, 81, 91
Lawlor, Thomas, 34
Lee, Joseph, 7, 8
Lehane, P.D., 89, 91
Lehenagh, 29, 48, 58
Leinster, 10, 12, 15, 17, 22

Lemass, Sean, 114
Liberties (Cork), 51, 54, 57, 58, 63, 88
Limerick City, 8, 10, 11
Limerick, Co., 8, 11, 15, 22, 27
Limerick Junction, 26
Limerick Rural Survey, 15
Liscarroll, 24, 54
Little Island ILLA, 36
Lixnaw, Co. Kerry, 45, 46
Lloyd George, David, 59
Local Government Board, 21
Local Government and Public Health, Department, Memorandum, 111
Louth, Co., 8, 11, 22
Lynch, Gilbert, 78, 81
Lyons, F.S.L., 7, 113

Mac Alleer, Paddy, 16
McCarthy, M.D., 114
McCeann, Richard, 81
Mac Entee, Sean, 90
Mac Gill, Patrick, 16
McGrath, Joseph, 17
McNabb, Patrick, 15, 19
Mac Swiney, Terence, 48, 54, 57

Macroom, 8, 11, 71
Mallow, 13, 71
Meath, Co., 8, 11, 12, 22
— 1922 Strike, 62
Meelin, 70
Midleton, 71
Minimum Wage, Factors in Determination of, 107-108
Mitchelstown, 13
Monaghan, Co., 10, 22
Moore, Sean, 85
Moynihan, Con, 16, 88, 89, 112
Mulcahy, Richard, 64
Munster, 10, 12, 15, 17, 22
Murphy, James, 35
Murphy, Patrick, FWUI, 75n, 112, 115
Murphy, T.J., 98

National Agricultural Association, 77, 79, 80
National Agricultural Labourers' Union, 24, 25

— *Irish* NALU, 24, 25
National Amalgamated Union of Labour, 45
National Farmers' Association, 114
National Farm Survey, 113
National Insurance Act 1911, 18
National Nutrition Survey, 14-15
National Union of Agricultural Workers, 79, 80, 81
National Wage Agreements, 17, 115-16
Neilan, P.J., 26
Newcastlewest, 15
Newtownsandes, Co. Kerry, Incident, 45
Norton, William, 90, 91, 98, 100, 105, 106

O'Brien, Kendal, 28
O'Brien, William (Home Rule), 27, 29 30
O'Brien, William, ITGWU, 34, 51, 66, 79
O'Cathain, Seamus, 15-16
O'Danachair, Caoimhin, 9
O'Donnell, Peadar, 15-16
O'Higgins, Kevin, 66-70
O'Leary, William (AWB), 105
O'Rahilly, Alfred, 89
O'Regan, Maurice, 70-72
O'Shannon, Cathal, 34
O'Shee, J.J., 28, 30, 31, 32
O'Sullivan, Florence, RDC, 37, 41

Old Age Pensions Act 1909, 18

Parnell, C.S., 117
Partridge, William, 31
Pattison, S., TD, 97
Phelan, Nicholas, 46
Pius XI, 108
Pollock, George, 81

"Quadragessimo Anno", 108

Raleigh, Timothy, 33
Red Flag, 41, 46, 54, 55, 59-60, 61, 67, 71, 118
Redmond, John, 27, 28

Referees, Court of, 97, 98
'Relatives Assisting', 7, 10
Rinneanna (Airport), 110
Road Workers (Co. Council), 20
Roberts, Ruaidhrí, 79
Roche, Paddy, 15, 16
Rochestown, Co. Cork, 54
"Rocks of Bawn", 15n
Ronayne, Michael, 105
Royal Irish Constabulary (RIC), 117
'Rural Exodus', 20
Russell, George (A.E.), 59
Ryan, Dr. James, Minister for Agriculture, 96, 101

'Servant Boys and Girls', 15, 16, 20
Sheehan, D.D., 26, 28, 29, 30, 31, 33
Sherlock, John, 81
Sinn Fein, 42, 47, 55
—Arbitration Courts, 52, 60, 61, 62
Slavery, 15, 82
Smith, Patrick, Minister for Agriculture, 89
Smyth, Michael, 78, 81, 90
Social Status, Labourers', 19-21
Social Welfare Act, 1952, 18
Social Welfare, Dept. of, First Report, 18
Special Infantry Corps and 1923 Waterford Strike, 68-9
"Standard, The", 75, 84-85
St. Mary's ILLA, 36
Strabane Fair, 16
Sullivan, John, 88
Supple, Christy, 66
Synnott, Nicholas J., 21

Tanner, Dr., 27
Tipperary, Co., 8, 11, 22, 27, 28
Tractors, 20
Trade Boards, 17, 104, 108
Tully, James, TD, 105-6, 114

Ulster, 10, 12, 15
Unemployment Assistance Act 1933, 18, 98
Unemployment Insurance Act 1920, 17

United Irish League, 30
Upper Glanmire ITGWU, 36

Vocational Organisation, Report of Commission, 109
"Voice of Labour", Attack on, 66

Wage Rounds, 1960s, 115
Wages Standstill Orders 1941-46, 110
War of Independence, 8, 56,
Waterford, Co., 8, 11, 22
— Farmers' Association, 69
— 1923 Farm Strike, 68-70, 72
"Waterford Plough and Furrow", 19
Wexford, Co., 8, 11, 22, 27
— Farmers' Association, 51
Whiteboys, 8
Whitechurch ILLA, 36
— ITGWU, 36
— 1919 Dispute, 48
— 1921 Strike, 60-61
Wicklow, Co., 8, 11, 22
Widgers, Joseph, 46
Wilson, Deputy, 66-67
Women Labourers, 7, 15, 16, 20
"Women Today" Radio Programme, 15n
Workers' Union of Ireland, Ch. 5*passim*
Workman's Compensation Act 1900, 18
Workmen's Houses, 20, 21
Working Conditions, Farm Labourers', 15-18
Wyndham Act, 27

Young, Joe, 16

Other Athol Books Publications
Summer 1988

A Story Of The Armada
by Captain Francisco De Cuellar, Joe Keenan and others

The Constitutional History Of Eire/Ireland
by Angela Clifford

Northern Ireland And The Algerian Analogy: A Suitable Case For Gaullism?
by Hugh Roberts

The Dubliner: The Lives, Times And Writings Of James Clarence Mangan
by Brendan Clifford

Thomas Russell And Belfast
by Brendan Clifford

The Veto Controversy, including Thomas Moore's **A Letter To The Roman Catholics Of Dublin** (1810)
by Brendan Clifford

The Life And Poems Of Thomas Moore
edited by Brendan Clifford

Available from
ATHOL BOOKS,
10 Athol Street,
Belfast, BT12 4GX.